LEARNING WORKS ENRICHMENT SERIES

EGYPTIANS
MAYA · MINOANS

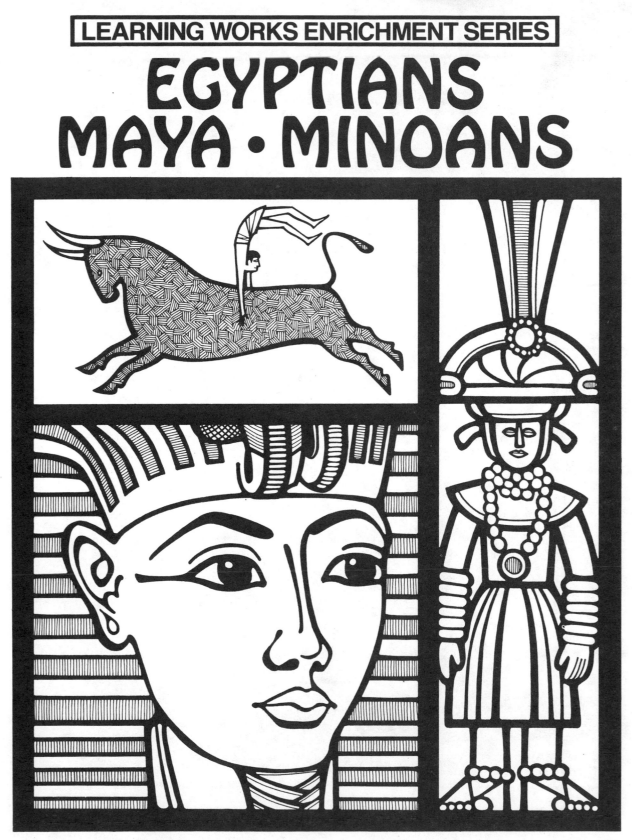

WRITTEN BY SUSANNA MATTHIES
ILLUSTRATED BY BEVERLY ARMSTRONG

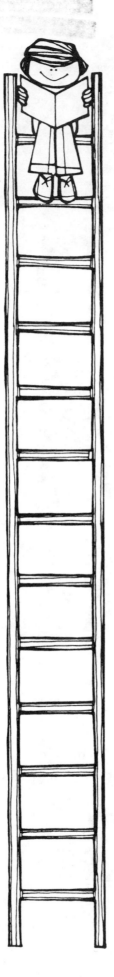

The Learning Works

Edited by Sherri M. Butterfield

The purchase of this book entitles the individual teacher to reproduce copies for use in the classroom.

The reproduction of any part for an entire school or school system or for commercial use is strictly prohibited.

No form of this work may be reproduced or transmitted or recorded without written permission from the publisher.

Contents

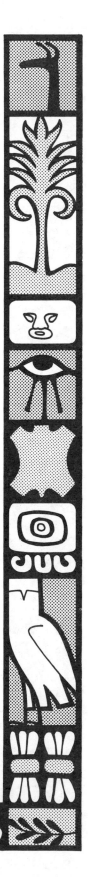

Contents
(continued)

To the Teacher

The activities in this book have been selected especially for gifted students in grades 4 through 8 and are designed to challenge them and to help them develop and apply higher-level thinking skills. These activities have been grouped into the following sections: Egyptians, Maya, and Minoans.

Egyptians

The ancient Egyptian civilization lasted more than three thousand years, longer than the span of history from the time of Alexander the Great until today. The relative stability of this civilization allowed unparalleled development in the areas of art, architecture, written language, and philosophy. Fortunately for us, time has not destroyed the monuments and messages which the ancient Egyptians left beside the Nile. In this section, students will encounter some of the people, thoughts, and innovations that made the ancient Egyptian civilization unique.

Some of the words in this section may, at first, appear mind-boggling or tongue-twisting. For this reason, you may wish to explain to your students that both the language spoken by the ancient Egyptians and the symbols used to represent it were very different from English. From what we can tell, this ancient language contained many consonant sounds and few vowel sounds. When messages written in Egyptian hieroglyphics were translated into English, every effort was made to make the words phonetically accurate, that is, to spell the sounds as they were once pronounced. But no one living today knows *exactly* how the ancient Egyptians spoke or, for that matter, how they pronounced the names of their pharaohs; therefore, when reading these often strange-looking names, students should be encouraged to say them just as they look. For example, the name **Hatshepsut** should be pronounced in three quick, equally emphasized syllables, each containing a short vowel, that is, **hăt-shĕp-sŭt.**

Maya

The Maya, ancient inhabitants of Mesoamerica, created one of the world's most advanced civilizations. They used hieroglyphic writing, made amazingly accurate astronomical observations, developed a complex calendric system, and used the idea of zero in their mathematical reckonings at least five hundred years before anyone else thought of it. In this section, students are introduced to these Stone Age artisans and to the mystery that still surrounds them.

Minoans

The Minoans were thought to be mythical until proof of their existence was discovered in A.D. 1900. Research since that time has established the island nation of Crete as Europe's first great civilization. In this section, students will meet some of the figures that peopled Minoan history and mythology, learn about the Minoans' accomplishments, and probe the mystery of their sudden disappearance.

In studying these three civilizations, you may wish to focus on the unique way in which each one met the individual needs that are common to all humanity. For instance, how did the Egyptians feed and shelter themselves and attempt to answer life's eternal questions? Was the Maya social structure more or less rigid than that of the Minoans? By studying the lives, thoughts, and accomplishments

To the Teacher
(continued)

of each culture, students can gain an understanding of the experiences they share with people of other times and places and an appreciation of the rich heritage that is theirs.

Within each of the three sections are bulletin board and learning center ideas, a pretest and a posttest, as many as thirty activity pages, detailed instructions for more than sixty activities, suggestions for additional correlated activities, an answer key, and an award to be given to students who satisfactorily complete the unit of study. These materials may be used with your entire class, for small-group instruction, or by individual students working independently at their desks or at learning centers. Although you may want to elaborate on the information presented, each activity has been described so that students can do it without additional instruction.

All of the activities within this book are designed to provide experiences and instruction that are qualitatively different and to promote development and use of higher-level thinking skills. For your convenience, these activities have been coded according to Bloom's taxonomy. The symbols used in this coding process are as follows:

KN	knowledge	recall of specific bits of information; the student absorbs, remembers, recognizes, and responds.
CO	comprehension	understanding of communicated material without relating it to other material; the student explains, translates, demonstrates, and interprets.
AP	application	using methods, concepts, principles, and theories in new situations; the student solves novel problems, demonstrates use of knowledge, and constructs.
AN	analysis	breaking down a communication into its constituent elements; the student discusses, uncovers, lists, and dissects.
SY	synthesis	putting together constituent elements or parts to form a whole; the student discusses, generalizes, relates, compares, contrasts, and abstracts.
EV	evaluation	judging the value of materials and methods given purposes; applying standards and criteria, the student judges and disputes.

These symbols have been placed in the left-hand margin beside the corresponding activity description. Usually, you will find only one symbol; however, some activities involve more than one level of thinking or consist of several parts, each involving a different level. In these instances, several symbols have been used.

Egyptians

Bulletin Board Ideas

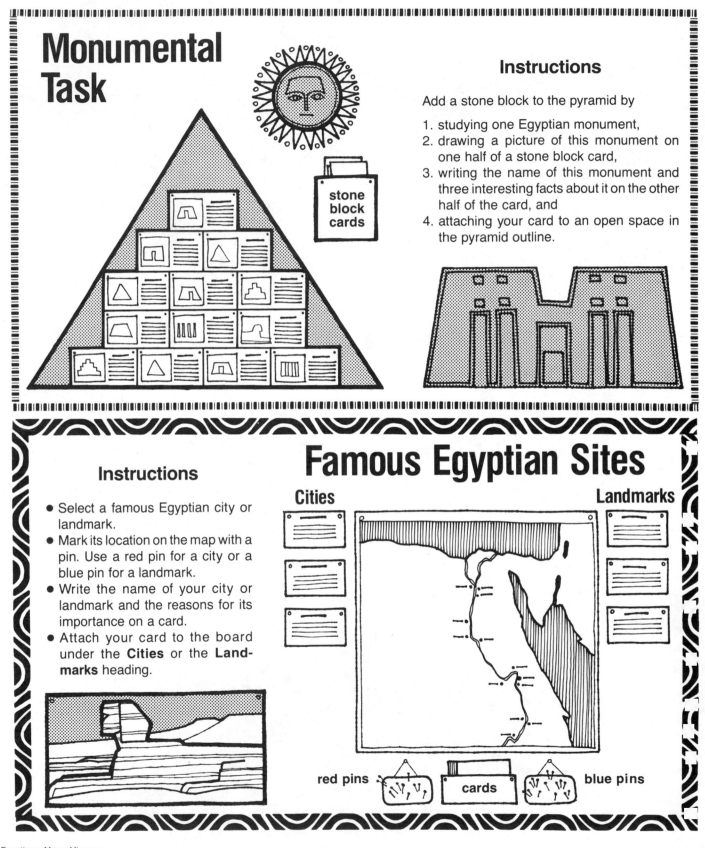

Monumental Task

Instructions

Add a stone block to the pyramid by

1. studying one Egyptian monument,
2. drawing a picture of this monument on one half of a stone block card,
3. writing the name of this monument and three interesting facts about it on the other half of the card, and
4. attaching your card to an open space in the pyramid outline.

stone block cards

Famous Egyptian Sites

Instructions

- Select a famous Egyptian city or landmark.
- Mark its location on the map with a pin. Use a red pin for a city or a blue pin for a landmark.
- Write the name of your city or landmark and the reasons for its importance on a card.
- Attach your card to the board under the **Cities** or the **Landmarks** heading.

Cities

Landmarks

red pins

cards

blue pins

Learning Center Ideas

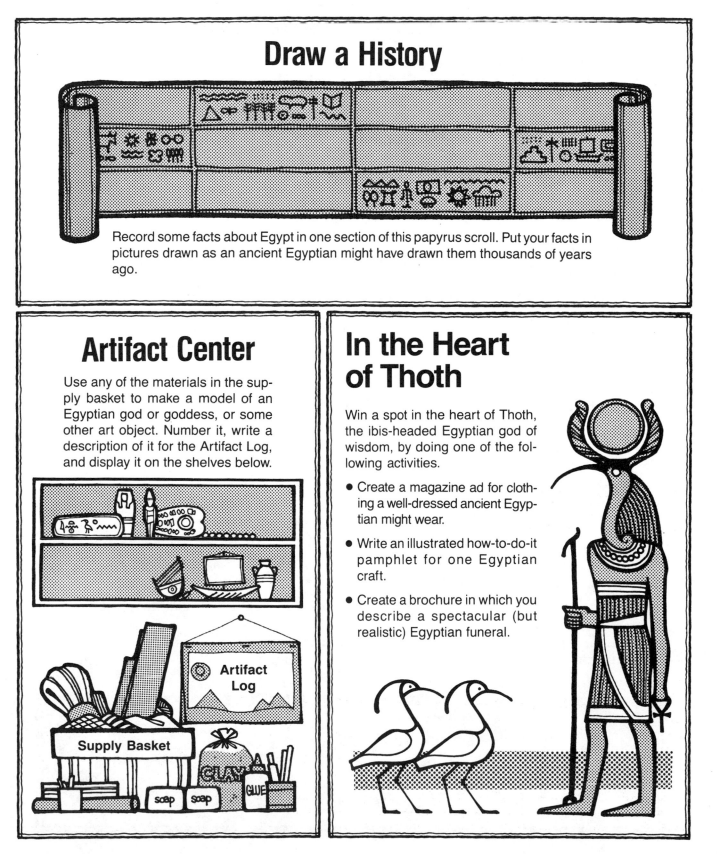

Draw a History

Record some facts about Egypt in one section of this papyrus scroll. Put your facts in pictures drawn as an ancient Egyptian might have drawn them thousands of years ago.

Artifact Center

Use any of the materials in the supply basket to make a model of an Egyptian god or goddess, or some other art object. Number it, write a description of it for the Artifact Log, and display it on the shelves below.

Artifact Log

Supply Basket

CLAY

soap   soap

GLUE

In the Heart of Thoth

Win a spot in the heart of Thoth, the ibis-headed Egyptian god of wisdom, by doing one of the following activities.

- Create a magazine ad for clothing a well-dressed ancient Egyptian might wear.

- Write an illustrated how-to-do-it pamphlet for one Egyptian craft.

- Create a brochure in which you describe a spectacular (but realistic) Egyptian funeral.

Name_____

Pretest

Circle the letter beside the best answer or the most appropriate response.

1. The ancient Egyptians inhabited the
   a. Fertile Crescent.
   b. Nile Valley.
   c. Tigris Valley.
   d. Nubian Desert.

2. Egypt is sometimes called
   a. the birthplace of democracy.
   b. the land of the rising sun.
   c. the land of the midnight sun.
   d. the gift of the Nile.

3. The ancient Egyptian economy was based on
   a. trade.
   b. production and sale of artwork.
   c. farming.
   d. mining.

4. The first Egyptian boats were made of
   a. wood.
   b. papyrus.
   c. clay.
   d. glass.

5. The Egyptians had to trade with other countries to obtain which one of the following building materials?
   a. stone
   b. mud-brick
   c. wood
   d. papyrus

6. Egyptian history is divided into how many kingdoms?
   a. two
   b. three
   c. five
   d. seven

7. Egypt was first made into one nation by
   a. King Narmer.
   b. Amenhotep IV.
   c. Tutankhamon.
   d. Ramses II.

8. Mummification was performed primarily
   a. to preserve the body.
   b. by magicians.
   c. at funerals.
   d. at parties.

9. The pyramids were built
   a. to impress visitors.
   b. to commemorate great events.
   c. to serve as tombs.
   d. to serve as objects of beauty.

10. The ancient Egyptian system of writing was based on small pictures that stood for words or ideas. These pictures are called
    a. petroglyphs.
    b. photographs.
    c. cryptographs.
    d. hieroglyphs.

Ancient Egypt

Before the time of recorded history, perhaps as many as ten thousand years ago, people settled in the valley of the Nile River where it flows through what is now Egypt. In this fertile land, they hunted and fished, herded and farmed. As their farms prospered, they were freed from the daily struggle to survive that enslaved many ancient peoples and were able to turn their considerable energies and talents toward creating and inventing. The result was a civilization that spanned more than three thousand years and produced many remarkable accomplishments. For example, these ancient Egyptians developed an effective system of writing, built enormous stone structures that are evidence of considerable engineering skill, and produced artwork that remains unsurpassed in its beauty.

The people who were responsible for these accomplishments lived comfortable, unvarying lives from one generation to the next. They believed that the gods had created a prosperous way of life for them, and they had no desire to change systems that had served them well. For this reason, their government, religion, and social structure remained essentially unchanged for as many as a thousand years at a time.

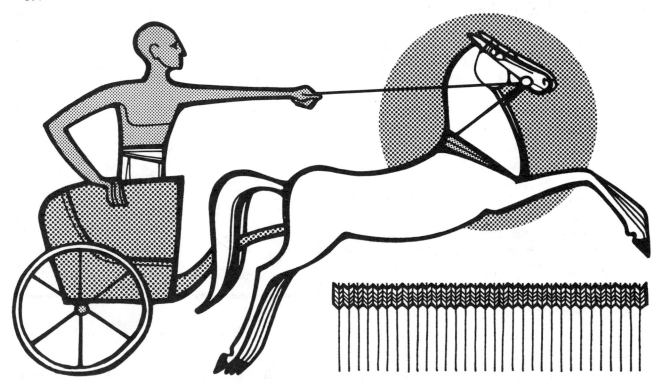

Activities

KN CO
1. Look at a map of the world or a globe. Find the continent of Africa. On this continent, find the Nile River. Trace this river from its source to its mouth. Through how many countries does it flow? Name them in order. Use the scale given on the map to estimate the length of this remarkable river.

SY EV
2. The government, religion, and social structure of ancient Egypt did change, but these changes occurred gradually, often over a period of five hundred or a thousand years. Compare the slow rate of change in ancient Egypt with the rapid rate of change in the modern world today. What effects might these vastly different rates of change have on the people who experience them? For example, would life in ancient Egypt have been more or less satisfying, stimulating, and stressful than life today? Explain your answers.

The Nile

Egypt is sometimes called "the gift of the Nile," a name that expresses its dependence on this river. The Nile River flows more than four thousand miles north across the continent of Africa from its headstream, the Kagera River between Tanzania and Uganda, to the Mediterranean Sea. Without the life-giving water it brings each year, Egypt's fertile Nile Valley would be dry and parched like the rest of this desert land; and life within it would be a constant struggle against hunger and thirst.

The lives of the ancient Egyptians revolved around the Nile. They settled on its banks, along the five-hundred-mile segment from Aswan to the Mediterranean Sea; and its rhythms regulated their lives. They captured the flooding waters of the river in irrigation basins and grew crops in the rich silt that it deposited. In addition, they made this river a thoroughfare for both travel and trade.

The Nile also played a role in the religion of the ancient Egyptians. One of their most worshiped gods was Hapi, god of the Nile. He, like the river he controlled, was the giver of all good. Thus, the Nile River made Egypt habitable, nurtured its crops, carried its commerce, and shaped its beliefs. At flood time, this river also idled Egypt's farmers, thereby producing a ready work force for construction of the temples and tombs that still stand beside the Nile's eternal waters.

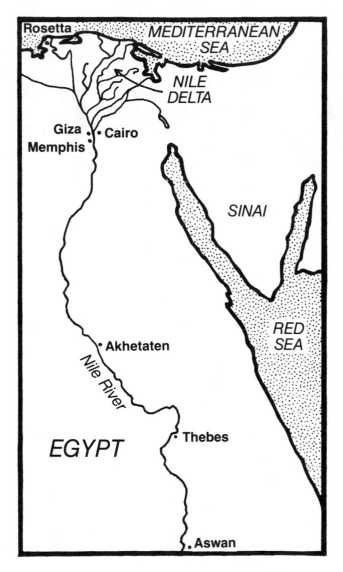

Activities

CO 1. Draw a detailed map of the Nile River from beginning to end. Mark and label important Egyptian sites.

AP 2. Design a fleet of boats and/or barges especially for travel on the Nile. Make your designs appropriate for the profile of the river they must navigate and for the products they must carry.

AN SY 3. The Mississippi, a major river in North America, flows from north to south, while the Nile, a major river in Africa, flows from south to north. Compare and contrast these two rivers with regard to their lengths, their uses, and the areas of land they drain, then describe the factor or factors that account for the difference in the direction of their flow.

SY 4. For the most part, the Nile flows gradually downhill, but it has six **cataracts,** or falls, where the water level changes abruptly and fast currents make it unnavigable. The most northerly of these cataracts is near Aswan. You decide to float on a raft down the river in late spring, when it is swollen with waters from melting snow. Write a story about your trip. On what portion of the river do you travel? How do you get safely past the cataracts?

Name_____

Egypt's History

For purposes of record keeping and discussion, historians have divided Egypt's long history into several periods and have cited particular accomplishments or events as marking the end of one period and the beginning of the next. Because these events took place thousands of years ago, the dates given for these periods are approximate and may vary somewhat from one source to another.

The first period in Egyptian history is the **Archaic Period**, which began about 3100 B.C., when Egypt was unified under its first king, Narmer. The second period, termed the **Old Kingdom**, began in 2686 B.C. and was the time when Egypt first became a great nation, built the pyramids, and established trade with its neighbors. For about fifty years, beginning in 2181 B.C., Egypt was ruled by rival pharaohs, and the political climate was unstable. This period of instability is termed the **First Intermediate Period.**

About 2133 B.C. Egypt was once again unified and grew rich and powerful. This prosperous period, known as the **Middle Kingdom**, lasted four hundred years, until the Egyptians were overpowered by Hyksos invaders. The Hyksos invasion is viewed as the beginning of the **Second Intermediate Period**, which lasted from 1633 to 1567 B.C. In 1567 B.C., a group of Egyptian princes drove out the Hyksos and ushered in the **New Kingdom**, Egypt's golden age of accomplishments, which lasted five hundred years and included the reigns of Amenhotep IV (also known as Akhenaton), Tutankhamon, Ramses II, and Ramses III.

The New Kingdom was followed by the **Third Intermediate Period** (*c.* 1085–751 B.C.), during which Egypt was divided and weak and sometimes ruled by Libyan and Nubian kings; the **Late Period** (*c.* 751–332 B.C.), during which Egypt was repeatedly invaded and conquered by Assyrians and Persians; and the **Ptolemaic Period**, which began when Alexander the Great conquered Egypt in 332 B.C. and ended with the Roman conquest in 30 B.C.

Activities

CO AP 1. After the New Kingdom, there were three more periods in Egypt's history. Do some research to learn more about major events and accomplishments during these periods. Then create a comic-book history of Egypt's last years. Add explanatory captions and/or dialogue as appropriate.

AP 2. Show the periods of Egyptian history and the major events that took place during each one on a color-coded time line.

SY 3. Compare your Egyptian time line with one for another civilization, either ancient or modern. In what ways are they alike? In what ways are they different?

EV 4. The ancient Egyptians lived according to one basic principle, which they believed was god-given. Find out what this principle was called and what it said. Then decide whether this principle is applicable today. Explain your decision.

King Narmer

A carved slate tablet found in Upper Egypt shows an important historical event. On it are depictions of a king engaged in victorious battle, subduing his enemies. This hero is Narmer, king of Upper Egypt, who has ended ages of armed conflict between the inhabitants of different areas of Egypt by conquering Lower Egypt and unifying the country. It is in 3100 B.C., with King Narmer and the unification, that Egypt's history really begins.

The slate tablet also shows the origin of the double crown, which all pharaohs after Narmer wore as one of the symbols of their office. On one side of the tablet, Narmer is shown wearing a tall, white, knobbed crown, which was the crown of Upper Egypt. On the other side of the tablet, he is shown wearing the red crown of Lower Egypt. As a symbol of the country's unification, King Narmer created the double crown by placing the tall, white crown of Upper Egypt inside the red crown of Lower Egypt.

Not much is known about King Narmer. Early Greek historians wrote of a king named Menes who, they said, had unified Egypt. They claimed that he then reigned for sixty-two years and that he was killed by a hippopotamus. Egyptologists have been unable to find a Menes listed among the known rulers of ancient Egypt and now believe that Menes and Narmer were two different names for one person.

Activities

KN CO 1. Draw and color a portrait of one of Egypt's great rulers. Below the portrait, print the ruler's name and list some of his most important accomplishments. Add your portrait to a classroom gallery entitled **Pharaohs' Portraits** or **Portraits of Greatness.**

AP 2. King Narmer wore a crown that symbolized the unification of two opposing regions, Upper Egypt and Lower Egypt. Create a banner, crown, or poster symbolizing the unification of two opposing countries, ideas, political groups, or athletic teams.

AP AN 3. You are a wartime correspondent in ancient Egypt. Write a news article in which you describe the feats of King Narmer or some other Egyptian ruler.

The God-Kings

To the ancient Egyptians, their ruler was both god and king, a descendant of the sun god, Ra. His power was absolute, and no one could question his decisions or repeal his judgments. He filled all governmental positions, such as those of lord chamberlain and vizier, with people of his own choosing. The land and people of Egypt were his to do with as he wished.

Special customs governed both the behavior of this ruler and the behavior of his subjects. Because the ruler was a god, no one was allowed to address him directly or to talk about him. Instead, people called him **pharaoh**, meaning "the Great House." In this way, they spoke of his palace, but not of his person. When in the pharaoh's presence, they knelt and bent forward, putting their heads on the floor. A pharaoh was allowed to marry only someone of similar rank. Because no one outside the pharaoh's family had divine blood, pharaohs were forced to marry their sisters or half-sisters.

Much of a pharaoh's costume of state was a visual sign of his power and of Egypt's history. He wore a double crown, which symbolized the unity of Egypt. As royal insignia, he carried both a crook and a whip. The crook, similar to that used by a shepherd, symbolized the pharaoh's duty to lead and protect his people. The whip, or flail, signified the pharoah's power over his subjects. At ceremonies, a pharaoh often wore a false beard as a symbol of his power as a man.

Activities

KN CO 1. Pharaohs had five titles. What were they and what was the correct order for their use?

KN CO SY 2. **Vizier** was an important governmental office in ancient Egypt. Find out what the duties of this office were. Then compare them with the duties of a prime minister or president. In what ways are they similar? In what ways are they different?

AP 3. As a pharaoh, what judgments might you make in the following cases?
   a. A Syrian calls you by name and speaks directly to you.
   b. Someone insults your sister.
   c. Your trusted vizier refuses to carry out a royal command.
   d. A foreign shepherd has found your crook and has been using it to herd his sheep. When captured and brought before you for questioning, he claims that he had no idea of its significance.

SY EV 4. Throughout history, many countries have been governed by rulers with absolute power. Find out who some of history's despots have been, compare them, and then rank them according to whether they used their power wisely or unwisely, beneficially or destructively.

Name_____

How the World Began

The ancient Egyptians told an interesting myth to explain the creation of the world. In this myth's cast of characters are the principal gods and goddesses that the Egyptians worshiped.

Ra, the sun god, had forbidden Nut, goddess of the sky, to marry Geb, god of the earth. Despite Ra's interdiction, Nut and Geb were secretly wed and lived together on earth. Thus, the earth was dark because earth and sky were so close together that there was no room for sun and air.

When Ra discovered the couple's disobedience, he ordered Shu, god of the air, to separate them. Shu created a violent wind that tore Nut away from Geb so that Shu could lift the sky goddess back into the heavens. Shu held Nut's arched body high above the earth, creating the firmament; and Ra attached stars to it.

Each day as Nut stretched above the earth, resting only on the tips of her fingers and toes, Ra walked over the curve of her body, bringing light to the earth from sunrise to sunset. After Ra had completed his journey, he allowed Nut to return to earth, bringing darkness with her descent.

Now Ra had also forbidden Nut to bear children in any month of the Egyptian year. Fortunately, Thoth, a moon god, won five extra days in a game with the moon. These days were not in any Egyptian year, but were added to the calendar, making a year 365 days long. Thoth gave the days to Nut so that she and Geb could have their children—Osiris, Isis, Set, and Nepthys—who became great gods of Egypt.

Activities

AP
AN
SY
1. Keeping this story in mind, pretend that you are an Egyptian priest. A child to whom you have told this story asks you how the moon was created and what causes earthquakes and shooting stars. How would you respond? Create a myth in the Egyptian style to explain these natural phenomena.

SY
EV
2. Plato, the Greek philosopher, said, "The law, like a good archer, should aim at the right measure of punishment." Do you think that Plato would have felt Ra hit or missed the target in his punishment of Nut and Geb? Explain your answer.

The Pyramids

In the desert along the west bank of the Nile River, stand more than eighty stone structures that have fascinated people for thousands of years. These amazing structures are the Egyptian pyramids. The pyramids were built as colossal tombs to protect the bodies, souls, and treasures of Egypt's pharaohs. They are especially amazing because the ancient Egyptians built them without using modern machinery or even a wheel.

Tombs of one sort or another were built in Egypt from the earliest days. At first, they were rectangular, mud-brick buildings, called **mastabas,** with a burial chamber and storage area. During the Third Dynasty (about 2700 B.C.), King Zoser asked his brilliant architect, Imhotep, to build a mastaba for him. By stacking increasingly smaller mastabas one atop another, Imhotep created a new architectural form, the **step pyramid.**

King Zoser's step pyramid was an imposing edifice. Although it stood more than two hundred feet high and had six levels, it was not the largest pyramid. The largest true pyramid was built around 2565 B.C. at Giza for Khufu, a pharaoh whom the Greeks called Cheops. Completed in twenty years, this pyramid has smooth sides, rather than steps. It covers more than thirteen acres of desert land and contains approximately 2,300,000 stone blocks.

During the New Kingdom, a new type of pyramid appeared. This pyramid was not constructed as a freestanding building. Instead, it was cut from limestone cliffs in a hidden valley near Thebes.

Activities

KN CO 1. Draw a cutaway picture of a typical mastaba and of a true pyramid. Label the parts of each.

KN CO 2. Imhotep was not only an architect but also a physician, a sage, and a counselor to King Zoser. Do some research to learn more about this remarkable ancient Egyptian. Share some of what you learn by designing a dust jacket for a book about his life or a poster advertising a movie based on his accomplishments.

CO AP 3. Construction of the pyramids was once a mystery, but archaeologists and Egyptologists have now developed a theory about how they were constructed. First, do some research to learn how the pyramids were built. Then, share what you have learned by drawing a comic strip depicting the steps followed and the methods used in their construction.

AP 4. As an overseer of pyramid construction, you need to hire workers. Design an application form and devise ten questions to ask applicants in an interview.

AP SY 5. Ancient Egyptian architects devised many methods for hiding or blocking the entrances to pyramids and the burial chambers within them. Invent a foolproof method of your own. Present your method to the class in a series of labeled diagrams.

What's in a Picture?

The ancient Egyptians valued records. To one of their gods, they entrusted the painstaking task of weighing souls and keeping accounts. Around 3200 B.C., they discovered how to make a writing material from papyrus. They also devised a system of symbols that enabled them to record thoughts and events.

At first, the ancient Egyptian system of writing was fairly simple. It was based on the use of **hieroglyphs,** or small pictures that stood for words or ideas. As this writing system evolved, the hieroglyphs came to represent sounds. Still later, the Egyptians put these sound-representing hieroglyphs together to form words very much as we do with letters of the alphabet. There is, however, one major difference between the modern English alphabet and the ancient Egyptian system of hieroglyphs: in the English alphabet, there are twenty-six letters; in the ancient Egyptian system of hieroglyphs, there were more than seven hundred characters.

For a long time, the Egyptians used hieroglyphs for all of their writing. Even after hieroglyphs were replaced for everyday use by a simpler system, they were still used to write sacred texts. Around 700 B.C., a cursive script called **demotic** gained widespread popularity. Hieroglyphs subsequently fell into disuse, and the Egyptians eventually forgot their meanings entirely.

Fortunately, scholars have been able to rediscover the meanings of ancient Egyptian hieroglyphs through a lucky find and some clever detective work. In 1799, a large stone was found near Rosetta, Egypt. This stone bore a message from an Egyptian king. Because this message was composed while the Greeks ruled Egypt, it was written in both Greek letters and Egyptian hieroglyphs. For years, however, no one was able to understand how the Egyptian message corresponded to the Greek one. Then, in 1822, a French Egyptologist named Jean François Champollion (1790–1832) discovered a way to match the names of Egyptian rulers, which appeared on the stone in both ancient Egyptian hieroglyphs and the Greek alphabet. This discovery enabled Champollion to equate the unfamiliar hieroglyphs with familiar Greek words and to translate the hieroglyphic message.

Activities

KN
CO
1. **Papyrus** is a sedge, or tufted marsh plant. It was so universally used in ancient Egypt that it became the hieroglyphic symbol for Lower Egypt and was a common motif in Egyptian art. Do research to discover some of the many ways in which the Egyptians used papyrus. Then share this information with your class by means of a poster or chart.

CO 2. Describe in detail how papyrus was made into writing material, or paper.

AP 3. What is a **cartouche**? First, look up the meaning of this word. Then, discover what use Champollion made of cartouches. Finally, design your own hieroglyphic designation and place it inside a cartouche.

AP 4. In some ways, a message written in hieroglyphs resembles a rebus. Both are combinations of pictures that stand for ideas and of symbols that stand for sounds, syllables, or words. Create a rebus about a person or event that was important in the history of ancient Egypt.

Name _____

Egyptian Temples

The ancient Egyptians credited the gods with having ordained and preserved their way of life. When Egyptian farmers were prosperous and Egyptian armies were victorious, Egyptian rulers were grateful. They showed their gratitude to these powerful and puzzling deities by rebuilding, enlarging, and embellishing their temples into magnificent palaces. The pharaohs especially wanted to win favor with the gods because these Egyptian rulers hoped to spend eternity in their divine presence. But in their construction efforts, these Egyptian rulers were far from humble and self-effacing. Although the temples they built were dedicated to the gods, the pharaohs used these magnificent structures as a means of commemorating for eternity their own brief earthly lives and glorious deeds.

Egyptian temples varied in design, but they were usually reached by means of a long road lined with towering sculptures, often sphinxes, and entered by means of a ceremonial gateway called a **pylon.** The temple itself was divided into three sections: an open **courtyard,** beyond which no common person could pass; a **hypostyle,** or many-columned hall, which priests and select officials might enter; and a **sanctuary,** which was the god's private apartment. Only the pharaoh and the highest-ranking priests were permitted to enter this sacred place. In addition to the courtyard, hypostyle, and sanctuary, most temples included side chambers, where objects used in services were stored, and outbuildings, which housed priests and priestesses, served as classrooms, or were used as workshops.

The most spectacular of the ancient Egyptian temples was the temple of Amon-Ra, king of the gods, at the religious complex of Karnak in Thebes. There, statues of victorious warlords peopled the grounds, painted reliefs adorned the walls, and hieroglyphic inscriptions on soaring columns reminded the gods of the deeds of the pharaohs.

Activities

KN
CO
1. What is a **sphinx**? What special qualities does this creature possess? Why were sphinxes chosen to serve as guardians of temples?

KN
CO
2. The pharaohs and their architects decorated temples with sculptures that had symbolic meaning. What sculptures appeared at Karnak? What was their significance or meaning?

CO
AP
3. Study one of Egypt's beautiful temples. Then pretend that you are a guide at that particular temple. Draw and label a map of it and write a monologue you might use to explain the temple's history, special features, and significance to visitors.

CO
AP
4. First, read about the duties of a temple priest or priestess. Then, pretend that you serve in a temple and write a letter or journal entry in which you describe one day's events.

Scribes

In ancient Egypt, there were no typewriters, printing presses, or photocopiers. Personal and governmental documents and correspondence had to be written or copied by hand. This tedious task was performed by scribes.

The English word **scribe** comes from the Latin noun *scriba*, which means "official writer" and is related to the Latin verb *scribere*, meaning "to write." Egyptian scribes were educated men, trained to read, write, and perform certain mathematical calculations and administrative tasks. These men were both respected and powerful. In fact, a well-trained and ambitious scribe might win appointment to any position he chose—priest of a temple, governor of a province, or advisor to the pharaoh.

The training necessary to become a scribe was arduous. Boys entered special schools at the age of five years and studied until they were sixteen. Discipline in these schools was very strict, and students spent long hours writing with reed brushes and ink. They were not allowed to write on paper. Instead, they used chips of broken pottery or clay tablets. Aspiring scribes learned how to write letters, copy reports, keep accounts, log taxes, and make mathematical and astronomical calculations.

Once trained, scribes could obtain secure, well-paid jobs. Some found work in the temples, writing prayers and rituals. Others became government officials, worked for the army, or managed estates. Still others became royal scribes. They helped the pharaoh and his staff keep court records and govern the country. They also wrote inscriptions and eulogies on temple or tomb walls.

Activities

KN CO
1. Scribes usually sat at desks in small rooms, called **scriptoriums**, and laboriously copied manuscripts by hand. In your classroom, set up a scriptorium. Make it a place where students can learn about different styles of writing and practice their penmanship.

KN CO
2. Think about the number of English words you know that are related to the Latin verb *scribere*, meaning "to write." For example, there are **scribble, scribe, script, scriptorium, inscribe, inscription, prescribe,** and **prescription.** First, list all of the words you can think of on a sheet of paper. Then, look up and write the meanings of these words beside them.

CO AP
3. Look through the Business Opportunities and Services Wanted sections of the classified ads in your local newspaper. Make a list of the positions advertised for which an Egyptian scribe would be qualified by his education, training, and experience.

CO AP
4. Scribes carried kits with all of the necessary writing implements. Find a picture or description of one of these ancient scribe's kits. Then, make a modern scribe's kit for yourself.

CO AP AN
5. The Egyptians, Greeks, and Romans all employed scribes to write their important documents and copy their books; and this practice continued during the Middle Ages and early Renaissance. Do some research to learn about the prevailing levels of education and technology during these times. Then use what you have learned to explain what inventions and events made the work of scribes obsolete.

Farming in Ancient Egypt

Ancient Egypt, a rich and prosperous nation, depended on farming for its livelihood. Products grown by farmers living in the fertile Nile Valley fed and clothed Egypt's people. These products were also its "money."

Early Egyptian farmers raised livestock—cattle, geese, oxen, and pigs. They planted wheat, which was universally needed for baking and feeding livestock, and flax, from which linen for clothing was made. They also grew a variety of vegetables and fruits, including dates, figs, grapes, and pomegranates.

These farm products were not only consumed but also traded and used for payment of taxes and wages. Farmers were expected to give portions of their crops, especially grain and livestock, to the government. Payment to workers on state construction projects was in food or livestock.

Most of the workers on the state projects were farmers. In June, when the Nile flooded, the farmers would break the dams on their irrigation canals, allowing the floodwaters to flow over their fields. While the fields were inundated, the farmers could not cultivate them, but they were far from idle. During this time, the farmers left their fields and went to work for the pharaoh. In November, when the waters had receded, the farmers returned to their farms to plow and plant crops that would be harvested in April.

Activities

CO AP 1. Long ago, the Egyptians invented a water-lifting device called a **shaduf.** First, locate a picture or diagram of one of these devices in a book about Egypt. Then, make a working model of a *shaduf* and demonstrate its use.

CO AP 2. Create a farmers' page for a newspaper that might have been published in ancient Egypt. Include appropriate advertisements, agricultural news, weather forecasts, and even some gossip.

AN SY EV 3. During the growing season, government tax officials visited each Egyptian farm to count livestock and estimate crop yield. On the basis of their calculations, they told each farmer what taxes he had to pay. As you might imagine, this system worked reasonably well if the crop grew as predicted, but not so well if there was a blight, a fire, or a drought. Pretend that you are a tax specialist in ancient Egypt. Devise a fairer and more flexible system of tax assessment, and prepare a detailed explanation of it for presentation to a government tax official.

Name_____

Ships and Trade

The ancient Egyptians made the Nile River a thoroughfare for both travel and trade, and they created a variety of craft to ply its waters. The earliest known picture of a boat depicts an Egyptian papyrus reed raft, which was poled or paddled along the Nile in Egyptian prehistory. Later, the Egyptians lashed bundles of reeds together to form cigar-shaped boats, tying the bundles at each end so that they came to a point and curved up toward each other. Boats of this kind were faster-moving than the simple reed rafts and are still in use today.

By the time of the Old Kingdom (*c.* 2686 B.C.), the Nile was jammed with boats and ships of one sort and another. Egypt was trading with countries along the Nile and across the Mediterranean Sea. Larger craft were needed to haul goods. Oval-shaped wooden boats with a single square sail and rows of long oars along both sides were used as cargo vessels. Barges also were used for trade, especially to haul the timber Egypt could not produce and was forced to import. These barges were sometimes as long as two hundred feet.

During the New Kingdom (*c.* 1567–1085 B.C.), Egyptian shipbuilding reached its peak, and vessels of every variety appeared. There were war galleys, wooden sailboats, funeral barges, hunting skiffs, fishing boats, and reed rafts. Wealthy Egyptians often had sailing fleets that included cargo ships, pleasure craft, and even kitchen boats, on which food was carried and prepared during their river outings.

Activities

KN CO 1. Hatshepsut, queen of ancient Egypt, built a magnificent temple on the west side of the Nile River at Deir el-Bahri near Thebes. On the walls of this temple were pictorial representations of a trading expedition to the African land of Punt. Investigate Queen Hatshepsut's voyage to this mysterious land. What country might Punt have been? What interesting or unusual things did Egypt obtain in its trade with this country?

CO AP 2. Imagine that you are a stowaway on an early Egyptian boat. What size is the boat? What does it look like? Where are you going? Why? How comfortable is your voyage? What misfortunes befall you? Keep a diary of your adventures so that you can share them with your grandchildren many years from now.

AP AN SY 3. The single square sail used by the Egyptians on their cargo ships made ocean sailing risky because vessels equipped in this way were difficult to turn. Build a model of one of these ships, test it in water, and then change its design to make it more maneuverable.

Homelife

As is true in most civilizations, how comfortably an Egyptian lived depended on his wealth. Most Egyptian paintings show the pleasant activities and beautiful surroundings enjoyed by members of the upper classes. Unfortunately, there is not much archaeological evidence regarding the homes and homelives of the ordinary people.

Wealthy Egyptians lived quite luxuriously. If they were city dwellers, they resided in three- or four-story mud-brick houses with expensive furniture and many servants. The affluent often owned large estates outside the cities. Surrounded by high walls, these estates were both self-contained and self-sufficient. In addition to a large house for the owner, they were comprised of animal pens, kitchens, storerooms, workshops, and servants' quarters, and could supply everything the residents needed, including food, fiber for clothing, and grain for family use or sale.

The inhabitants of these estates spent their free time relaxing with family members and entertaining friends. They gave parties, dances, and feasts, often in the private gardens of their homes. On these gala occasions, children splashed in the garden pools and played tug-of-war, while adults talked or played senet. Sometimes families went on picnics and river outings together.

In the hot season, Egyptians, whether they lived in one-room huts or in huge villas, used their roofs as patios. After the sun went down, they sought respite in the evening air from the stifling indoor heat. Apparently, the small windows in Egyptian houses, though placed near the ceilings to catch any passing breezes, were not sufficient to cool the homes in this sweltering desert land.

Activities

KN CO 1. What kind of game was **senet**? Do some research to discover how it was played and what modern game or games it resembles.

CO AP 2. Ancient Egypt was a hot, dry, desert land without rainfall or electricity. Draw and label plans for an Egyptian house that would heat slowly and cool quickly. Consider such factors as insulation and air circulation.

AP 3. Design a reasonable cooling system for an ancient Egyptian house.

CO AP 4. Create a catalog of ancient Egyptian furnishings. Include both illustrations and descriptions.

CO AP 5. The ancient Egyptians wore distinctive clothing and makeup. Draw pictures of the Man of the Year and Woman of the Year as they might have appeared on the pages of an ancient Egyptian fashion magazine entitled *Nile*.

SY EV 6. Compare the rights of women in ancient Egypt with the rights of women in modern Egypt. In what ways are they alike? In what ways are they different? If you were a woman, in which Egypt would you rather live? Explain your answer.

Mummification

The ancient Egyptians believed strongly in the life of the soul after the death of the body. They also believed that, to ensure the eternal life of the soul, it was necessary to preserve the body as a home for it. **Mummification** is the lengthy and complex process used by the ancient Egyptians to preserve the body after death so that it might house the soul in the afterlife. This process was both art and rite. It recreated the myth of Osiris, the slain god whose mate and sister Isis skillfully wrapped his dismembered corpse and restored it to life at her side.

Egyptian mummification took seventy days. After death, a body was taken to the embalmer's shop, where the brain was drawn through the nose with a wire hook, and all other vital organs except the heart were removed. The disembodied organs were preserved in **canopic jars,** ornate covered vessels made especially for this purpose. For several weeks, the body was allowed to soak in a tub of preserving salt, called **natron.** Then it was removed from the tub, dried, and rubbed with fragrant oils, wines, and spices. Next, the empty internal spaces were packed with linen, and the body was wrapped heavily with linen strips. Finally, the head was covered with its portrait mask, and the body was placed in a coffin for its journey to the next world.

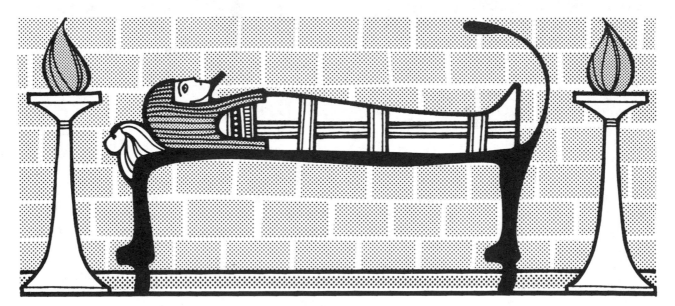

Activities

co 1. If you have an interest in chemistry, do research to discover what **natron** is, what elements it contains, how to write its chemical formula, and some other ways in which it has been used.

co 2. The Egyptians believed strongly in an afterlife. Take a survey among your friends and/or the members of your family to determine what they believe about death and life afterward. Share your findings with the class by means of a chart or graph.

AP
SY 3. Anubis was the Egyptian god of embalming. First, imagine what this deity might look like and draw a picture of him. Then, look up a picture of Anubis as the ancient Egyptians portrayed him. Compare your drawing with the Egyptian one. In what ways are they similar? In what ways are they different?

SY 4. Select two or three other cultures, ancient or modern. Do some research to learn about the customs that surrounded death and burial in these cultures. Compare these customs with the customs and practices of the ancient Egyptians. In what ways are they similar? In what ways are they different? What factors might account for the similarities and differences you have observed?

Name_____

Journey to the Kingdom of the Dead

The ancient Egyptians spent a lot of money and energy holding funerals, building tombs, and stocking burial chambers with comforts and treasures. At first, one might think that they feared death and were trying, through some artificial means, to escape its reality; but nothing could be further from the truth. The Egyptians were motivated not by fear but by their firm belief in the possibility of a pleasant life after death and their fervent desire to be prepared for it.

The ancient Egyptians believed that, before reaching a final resting place, both body and soul made a series of journeys. The first of these journeys was to the embalmer's shop, where the body was mummified so that it and the soul that dwelled within it would not be destroyed before they reached the relative safety of the tomb. The second of these journeys was from the embalmer's shop to the tomb. The mummy was hauled from the shop to its final resting place by means of a funerary sledge drawn by oxen and was accompanied on this journey by a lavish funeral procession. Within the tomb, the burial chamber, where the body would rest, reflected years of elaborate preparation. Painted scenes adorned its walls; fine furniture, good food, and treasures for the dead to enjoy lay within. Before priests placed the body in a stone box, called a

sarcophagus, they performed a ceremony to restore the powers of the dead person to breathe, move, and eat so that he or she could savor the tomb's delights. Finally, when all was in readiness, the tomb was sealed.

With the body thus at rest, the three souls, or three parts of the soul, began their journeys. The *ka*, which is best understood as a person's life force, remained in the tomb to experience the luxuries there; the *ba*, a birdlike spirit, was free to fly anywhere it wanted; and the *akh,* a ghostlike spirit, began its pilgrimage from the land of the living to the kingdom of the dead. The soul was aided on this terrifying journey by talismans placed on its mummy and by passwords written on the indispensable Book of the Dead, with which it had been furnished.

At last the soul reached the Halls of Double Justice, where Anubis, the jackal-headed guardian of the dead, weighed it against a feather, the ideogram of Maat and symbol of truth. If the soul was innocent and pure, the scale balanced, and the soul was released to mingle freely with the gods and the spirits of the dead. If the soul was evil and heavy with guilt, it tipped the scale and was devoured by the hybrid monster Amemait. Thus, only the good were able to complete all of the journeys successfully and reach eternal life.

Activities

KN
CO

1. Do some research to learn what gods were associated with the Egyptian kingdom of the dead.

SY

2. If you sat on the panel of the forty-two judges, a group whose members were responsible for examining souls regarding the worth of their lives, what questions would you ask? List ten questions and number them to indicate their importance.

SY

3. Compare the ancient Egyptian process of **mummification** with the modern technique known as **cryonics.** In what ways are these two processes and the beliefs associated with them similar? In what ways are they different?

A Falcon on Its Perch

The Greek word *pantheios* means "of all gods." From this Greek word comes the English word **pantheon,** the name given to the officially recognized gods of a people.

The Egyptian pantheon included a large number of gods and goddesses. These deities controlled all of the forces of nature—sun, wind, rain, and tides—and held man's fate in their hands. In addition, some of these divine beings represented certain concepts, ideas, or values. For example, Thoth was patron of science and literature, wisdom and invention. He served as spokesman for all of the gods and was keeper of their records. But not all Egyptian gods and goddesses represented good qualities. For example, the goddess Sekhmet was a powerful and savage patron of battle and war who delighted in human carnage.

In Egyptian art, gods and goddesses were often represented as having a human body but the head of the animal with which they were most closely associated. For instance, Thoth had the head of an ibis, and Sekhmet had the head of a lion. Anubis, the god of the dead, had the head of a jackal.

Some members of the ancient Egyptian pantheon were more important than others and remained prominent throughout most of ancient Egypt's lengthy existence. Among the more important deities was Ra, the sun god, who appeared at different times under different names and eventually became Amon-Ra, king of the gods. Other deities who were important to the ancient Egyptians were Osiris, god of the dead; Isis, wife of Osiris and kindly protector of children; and Horus, son of Osiris and Isis, who is represented in Egyptian art by a falcon or by a falcon-headed being.

Many ancient Egyptians thought of the sky as a divine falcon whose two eyes were the sun and the moon. Because of this association, the hieroglyph they developed to represent the idea of god was a falcon on its perch.

Activities

CO
AP
1. People who have little or no scientific knowledge often create myths to explain natural occurrences. The ancient Egyptians, awed by the rising sun and grateful for the flooding Nile, developed imaginative stories to explain these events. They worshiped Hapi, god of the Nile, as the giver of all good; and through their storytelling, they turned the sun's journey across the sky into Ra's walk over the curve of Nut's body. Pretend that you are an ancient Egyptian who does not understand what causes the sun to glow hot or the wind to blow relentlessly across the desert sands. Create a myth to explain one or both of these natural phenomena.

AN
SY
2. Many ancient peoples, including the Egyptians, the Greeks, and the Romans, have associated particular animals and attributes with the members of their pantheons. In this context, **attributes** are objects that are closely associated with or belong to a specific god or goddess and are often used in paintings or sculpture to identify that deity. What animal and attribute would you associate with each of the following deities: Goddess of Laughter, God of Loyalty, God of Strength, God of Wisdom? Explain your answers.

History's First Great Queen

During the New Kingdom, around 1515 B.C., an extraordinary event occurred in Egypt. A woman established herself as ruler of that ancient land. This woman was Hatshepsut.

Though the rightful heiress to Egypt's throne, Hatshepsut was not permitted to rule because she was a woman, and Egyptian law forbade a woman's becoming pharaoh. For this reason, Hatshepsut's husband was made pharaoh. He soon died, leaving his young son to rule. Ignoring the boy's claim to the throne, Hatshepsut proclaimed herself ruler of Egypt and adorned herself with the traditional emblems of that office, including the ceremonial beard, a symbol of masculine power.

Hatshepsut reigned for eighteen years and distinguished herself as a strong and capable ruler. She established and kept peace in the country. She selected exceptionally talented men as aides, and commissioned them to improve Egypt's economy. She launched many trade expeditions, including one to the land of Punt, from which Egyptian sailors brought back such exotic objects as cosmetics, ebony, incense, ivory, leopard skins, monkeys, myrrh trees, and slaves. She urged artists and craftsmen to improve their skills and supported them by providing steady work. Under Hatshepsut's direction, the architect Senmut produced one of the finest monuments in Egyptian history, the Temple of Queen Hatshepsut, to glorify forever the name of history's first great queen and Egypt's woman-king.

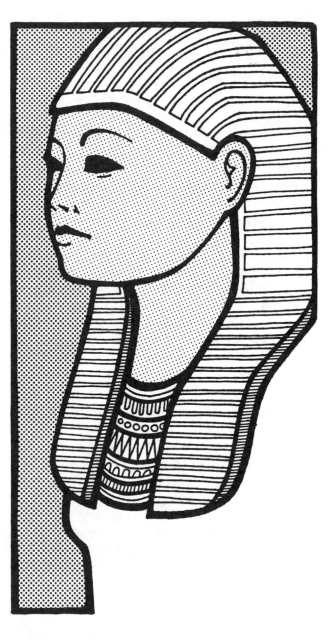

Activities

KN
AP
1. Do some research to learn what made Queen Hatshepsut's temple exceptional. Then, make a floor plan, sketch, or model of this temple and its site.

AN
SY
2. If you had walked through Hatshepsut's Egypt, you would have seen the word **Amon** written everywhere. Amon was the chief god during most of the New Kingdom (c. 1567–1085 B.C.). Imagine a stranger's walking through your country. List some of the places he or she might see the word **God** written. What assumptions might the stranger make about the religious beliefs of your country?

Name_____

He Who Served Aten

Amenhotep IV was a pharaoh with revolutionary ideas who took Egypt in many new directions. After Amenhotep began his reign (*c.* 1370 B.C.), he founded a new capital, made radical changes in Egyptian religion, and encouraged equally drastic changes in Egyptian art.

Amenhotep was deeply religious. Unlike other Egyptians, who believed in many gods, he believed in only one, Aten. Aten was represented in Egyptian art as a solar disk from which descended rays that terminated in hands. To those who worshiped him, Aten was the giver of light and the source of all life.

In honor of Aten, this Egyptian king changed his name from Amenhotep (meaning "Amon is satisfied") to Akhenaton (meaning "He who serves Aten"). He established Aten as the chief god of Egypt and sent workmen throughout the country to erase other gods' names from all buildings and to replace them with Aten's. Akhenaton abandoned the capital of Egypt at Thebes, a city dedicated to Amon, and established another in honor of Aten. Called Ahketaten, this city was built around the magnificent Temple of the Sun's Disk and contained spacious gardens, sparkling lakes, magnificent palaces, and luxurious villas.

During Akhenaton's rule, aesthetic taste changed also. Paintings and sculptures realistically portrayed people who were informally posed or engaged in everyday activities, a style that departed sharply from traditional, more formal Egyptian art. Akhenaton, himself, seems to have submitted willingly to this less formal style and, perhaps, to have encouraged it. In fact, there are some pictures of him and his family that are too informal and realistic to be flattering.

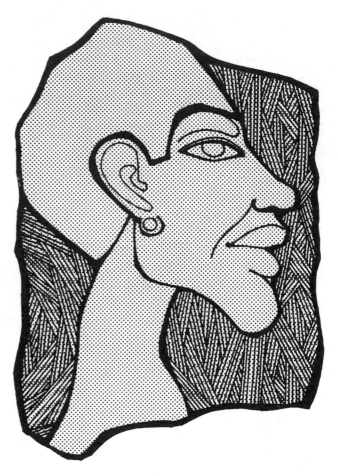

Many Egyptians were angered by Ahkenaton's changes. Soon after his death, his magnificent city was abandoned, Aten's name was erased, and the old gods were reinstated. Akhenaton's successor even changed his own name from Tutankhaten (meaning "living image of Aten") to Tutankhamon (meaning "living image of Amon").

Activities

KN CO 1. Egypt has had many capitals. Draw a map of Egypt on which you show the names and locations of its capitals. Date or color code them to indicate the periods of their active use.

AP 2. An **epithet** is a characterizing word or phrase used with or in place of the name of a person. For example, Eric the Red is an epithet. Think of several epithets that would be appropriate for Ahkenaton or for other rulers of ancient Egypt.

SY 3. Ahkenaton and his wife Nefertiti had six daughters. Imagine a conversation between Ahkenaton and one or more of his daughters. What might they discuss—politics, religion, art, or fashion trends? Write the scene you have imagined.

Correlated Activities

Art

KN CO The style of Egyptian art changed very little over thousands of years. Do some research to discover what factors limited the freedom of artists to express themselves and contributed to this uniformity.

KN CO What was the Village of Craftsmen? Find out what life in this village was like.

AP SY Create two paintings, one in the traditional Egyptian style and the other in the revolutionary Amarna style associated with Akhenaton.

Language Arts

KN CO Alone, with a partner, or as a member of a group, write each of the terms listed below on a separate three-inch-by-five-inch index card.

attribute	mummification
canopic jar	natron
cartouche	obelisk
flail	scarabaeus
hectare	senet
hieroglyph	*shaduf*
hypostyle	sistrum
ibis	talisman
ideogram	uraeus
mastaba	vizier

Look up the correct definition for each term. Make up two incorrect definitions for each term. Write all three definitions on the card below the term. Number the definitions and vary their order so that the first one is not always the correct one. For keying, write the number of the correct definition on the back of each card. When you have finished making the cards, challenge other individual students or groups to look at the cards and see how quickly they can match the terms with their correct definitions.

AP Make up riddles or hinky-pinkies based on information about ancient Egypt. A hinky-pinky consists of a question and its answer. The question may be in any form, but the answer must be a two-word rhyme in which both words have the same number of syllables. For example,

Question: What do you call the vegetables that Hatshepsut ate?
Answer: queen's greens

Question: What do you call tufted marsh plants belonging to the Egyptian god of the dead?
Answer: Osiris's papyruses

Correlated Activities
(continued)

SY   Create a myth explaining the yearly flood of the Nile River.

SY   Write a play, poem, or short story about your imaginary adventures on one of the pharaoh's hippopotamus hunts.

CO SY   Pretend that you are a travel agent. Plan a tour for present-day people who appreciate the art and history of ancient Egypt. Create and/or assemble a package of brochures, maps, and posters explaining your tour in detail.

Research

CO AP   What kind of calendar did the ancient Egyptians use? Make one.

KN CO   Find out about Hatshepsut's City of the Dead. Does it sound ghoulish to you?

KN CO   Do some research to learn more about ancient Egyptian construction techniques. What tools did the ancient Egyptians use? How did they make mud-brick? How did they quarry and transport huge stones? How did they move and erect obelisks?

AN EV   A new theory suggests that many of the blocks used by the ancient Egyptians for their monumental construction projects may not have been stone, which they hauled overland, but a concrete-like material, which they formed at the construction site. Do research to find out more about this theory. Then evaluate it to decide whether you agree or disagree. Explain the reasons for your decision.

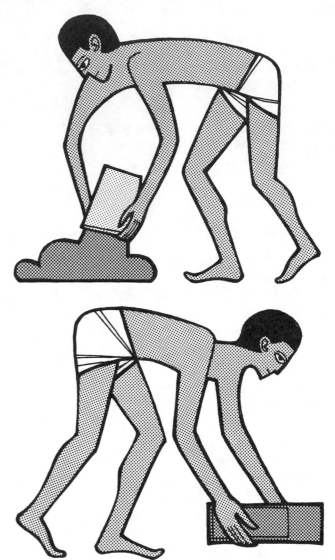

Answer Key

Pretest, Page 10		Posttest, Page 31	
1. b	6. b	1. c	6. c
2. d	7. a	2. a	7. b
3. c	8. a	3. d	8. d
4. b	9. c	4. b	9. a
5. c	10. d	5. c	10. b

Name_____

Posttest

Circle the letter beside the best answer or the most appropriate response.

1. The part of the Nile that the ancient Egyptians inhabited was
   a. all four thousand miles.   c. the northern five hundred miles.
   b. the southern five hundred miles. d. the cataract region.

2. The period in Egyptian history that began when Egypt was unified by its first king is called the
   a. Archaic Period.   c. Middle Kingdom.
   b. Old Kingdom.   d. New Kingdom.

3. The double crown worn by King Narmer and all pharaohs after him symbolized
   a. the ruler's identity as both god and king.
   b. the ruler's power to rule and duty to protect.
   c. the ruler's power as a man.
   d. the unification of Upper and Lower Egypt.

4. Ra was
   a. a birdlike spirit.   c. a king of Egypt.
   b. the god of the sun.   d. a queen of Egypt.

5. The largest true pyramid was built at Giza for
   a. King Zoser.   c. Khufu (Cheops).
   b. Tutankhamon.   d. King Narmer.

6. Of the plants listed below, which one was **not** grown easily, or in abundance, in ancient Egypt?
   a. grape vines   c. trees
   b. flax   d. wheat

7. A **cartouche** is
   a. a ceremonial headdress worn by pharaohs.
   b. an oval or oblong figure enclosing an Egyptian ruler's name.
   c. a monument to the Egyptian god Caraton.
   d. a boat built especially for travel on the Nile.

8. A **hypostyle** is
   a. a small picture that stands for a word or idea.
   b. a water-lifting device invented by the ancient Egyptians.
   c. a small room within an Egyptian temple used for writing.
   d. a many-columned hall within an Egyptian temple.

9. According to Egyptian mythology, the worthiness of souls was determined by weighing them against
   a. a feather.   c. papyrus.
   b. a stone.   d. wood.

10. An ancient Egyptian woman became history's first great queen. What was her name?
   a. Ahkenaton   c. Nefertiti
   b. Hatshepsut   d. Tutankhamon

This is to certify that

_____

(name of student)

has satisfactorily completed a unit of study
on the

Ancient Egyptians

and has been named

an

Honorary Egyptologist

in recognition of this accomplishment.

_____

(signature of teacher)

_____

(date)

Maya

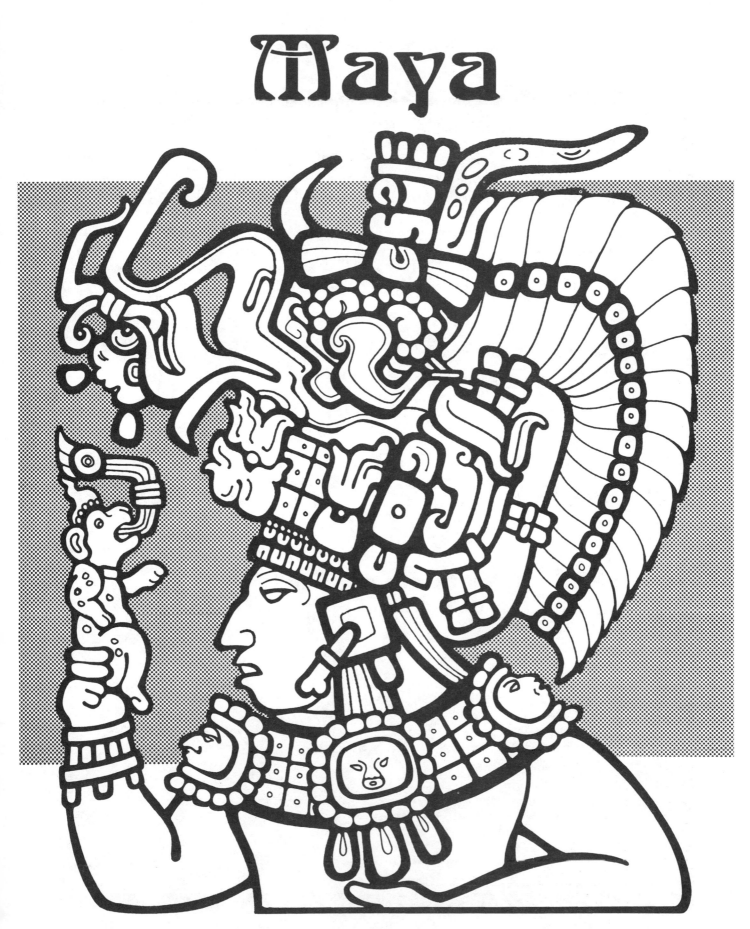

Bulletin Board Ideas

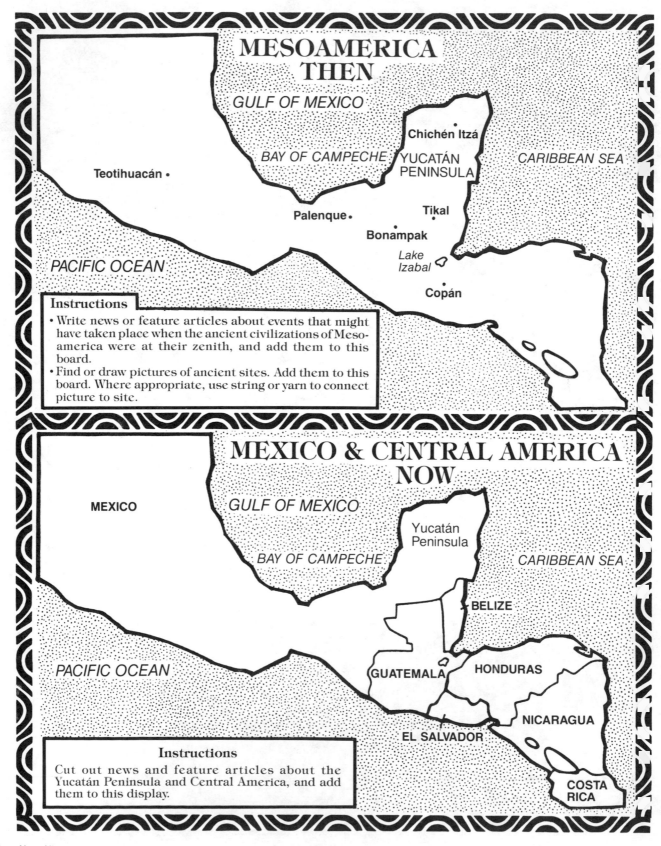

MESOAMERICA THEN

GULF OF MEXICO

Chichén Itzá

BAY OF CAMPECHE YUCATÁN PENINSULA

CARIBBEAN SEA

Teotihuacán •

Palenque •

Tikal •

Bonampak •

Lake Izabal

PACIFIC OCEAN

Copán •

Instructions

- Write news or feature articles about events that might have taken place when the ancient civilizations of Mesoamerica were at their zenith, and add them to this board.
- Find or draw pictures of ancient sites. Add them to this board. Where appropriate, use string or yarn to connect picture to site.

MEXICO & CENTRAL AMERICA NOW

MEXICO

GULF OF MEXICO

Yucatán Peninsula

BAY OF CAMPECHE

CARIBBEAN SEA

BELIZE

PACIFIC OCEAN

GUATEMALA HONDURAS

EL SALVADOR NICARAGUA

COSTA RICA

Instructions

Cut out news and feature articles about the Yucatán Peninsula and Central America, and add them to this display.

Learning Center Idea

Build Your Own Maya Temple-Pyramid

Complete the activity described on each terrace.
Display your work for other class members to enjoy.

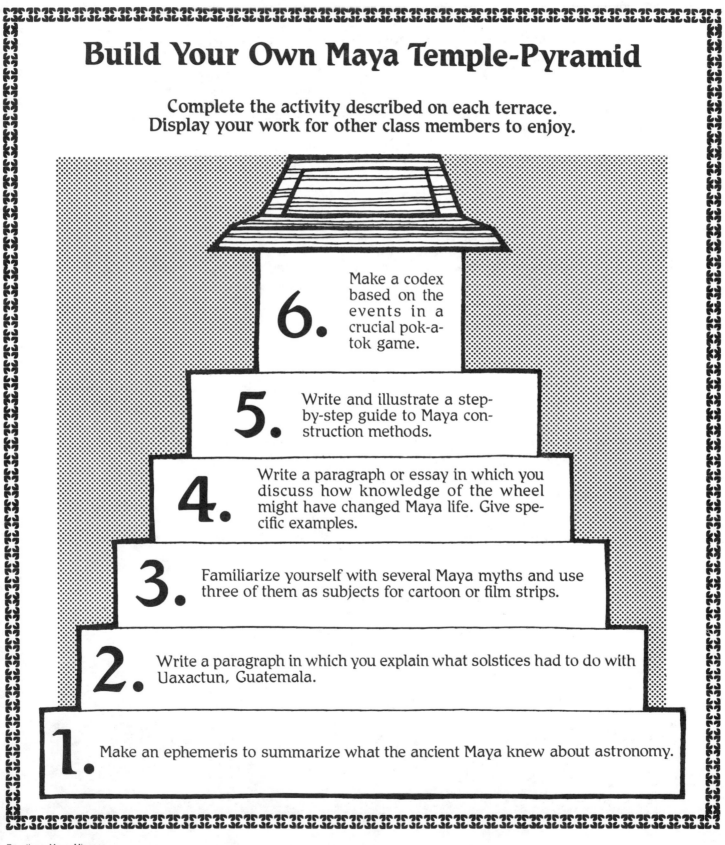

6. Make a codex based on the events in a crucial pok-a-tok game.

5. Write and illustrate a step-by-step guide to Maya construction methods.

4. Write a paragraph or essay in which you discuss how knowledge of the wheel might have changed Maya life. Give specific examples.

3. Familiarize yourself with several Maya myths and use three of them as subjects for cartoon or film strips.

2. Write a paragraph in which you explain what solstices had to do with Uaxactun, Guatemala.

1. Make an ephemeris to summarize what the ancient Maya knew about astronomy.

Pretest

Circle the letter beside the best answer or the most appropriate response.

1. The remarkable Maya civilization developed and flourished over a period of nearly three thousand years. During which of these periods did it exist?
   a. 8000–5000 B.C.
   b. 5000–2000 B.C.
   c. 2000 B.C.–A.D. 900
   d. 1000 B.C.–A.D. 1985

2. According to the theory presently accepted by archaeologists, the ancestors of the ancient Maya came from
   a. Asia.
   b. Egypt.
   c. the lost continent of Atlantis.
   d. the lost tribes of Israel.

3. The Maya inhabited a geographic area now known as
   a. North America.
   b. Mesoamerica.
   c. South America.
   d. the Yucatán Peninsula.

4. This area included what are now
   a. Campeche and Quitana Roo.
   b. Brazil and Argentina.
   c. Mexico and Central America.
   d. Canada and the United States.

5. Copán, Palenque, and Tikal were
   a. powerful Maya chiefs.
   b. explorers who located Maya ruins.
   c. important Maya deities.
   d. centers of Maya civilization.

6. The ancient Maya were conquered by
   a. the Spaniards.
   b. the Olmecs.
   c. Christopher Columbus.
   d. the jungle.

7. After the conquest, the descendants of the ancient Maya all but disappeared. The ruins of their remarkable cities were discovered during the nineteenth century by
   a. Meriwether Lewis and William Clark.
   b. John Lloyd Stephens and Frederick Catherwood.
   c. David Livingstone and Henry M. Stanley.
   d. Christopher Columbus and Francisco Córdoba.

8. In the development of their unique culture, the Maya were influenced by
   a. the Egyptians.
   b. the Minoans.
   c. the Greeks.
   d. the Olmecs.

9. Which trio of crops formed the basis of Maya agriculture?
   a. beans, corn, and squash
   b. flax, grapes, and wheat
   c. bananas, coconut, pineapple
   d. ginger root, rice, and soybeans

10. Which one of the following things was neither developed nor used by the Maya?
    a. a sophisticated calendar system
    b. a written language
    c. a potter's wheel
    d. a large pantheon

Name_____

A Lost Civilization

Have you ever heard of a lost civilization? Hidden in the undergrowth of Southern Mexico and Central America are the remains of one— that of the Maya—a civilization that flourished for more than two thousand years and then mysteriously came to an abrupt end at the height of its glory.

The Maya civilization began to develop around 2000 B.C. At that time, the people of Mesoamerica (a geographic area that includes the southern part of Mexico and the northern part of Central America) abandoned the nomadic life-style of hunters and gatherers to pursue a more settled, agricultural way of life. They tamed wild corn, grew a variety of crops, used hieroglyphic writing, developed a complex system of calendars that enabled them to predict eclipses, played a ritual ball game that was a metaphor for cosmic motion, and used the idea of zero in their numerical system at least five hundred years before anyone else had thought of it.

Although the Maya were essentially a Stone Age people, they formed clay dishes and figurines, carved statues, practiced weaving and other crafts, built temple-pyramids and palaces, and

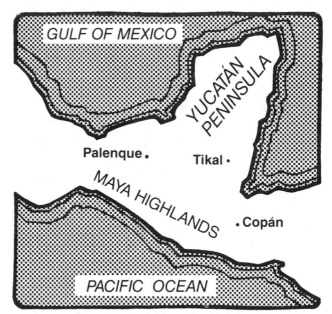

exchanged goods and ideas in their bustling marketplaces. Their knowledge of medicine was superior to that of any other civilization of their time; however, despite their many remarkable accomplishments, by A.D. 900, the Maya had vanished, leaving the southern centers of their civilization—Copán, Palenque, and Tikal—to be gradually reclaimed by the surrounding rain forest.

Activities

KN CO
1. Start a dictionary of terms that are related to the study of ancient civilizations. You may wish to include the following terms and their definitions :

archaeologist	codex	excavation	New World
artifacts	corbel	hieroglyphics	Old World
cenote	culture	Mesoamerica	pyramid

KN CO
2. Look at a map of Mesoamerica. On it locate the Yucatán Peninsula, the Maya lowlands, the Maya highlands, and the ancient Maya centers of Copán, Palenque, and Tikal.

KN CO
3. Make a time line showing the periods of existence for the ancient Egyptian and Maya civilizations and some of their important accomplishments.

SY
4. As far as we know, there was no contact between the ancient Egyptian and Maya civilizations. The similar discoveries they made and processes they developed were parallel accomplishments; that is, each civilization achieved separately, without the knowledge, influence, or aid of the other. Using the time line you made (activity 3), compare the longevity and accomplishments of these two civilizations. In what ways are they similar? In what ways are they different? If there was, in fact, no exchange of information and ideas between these civilizations, what factors might account for the similarities?

Name_____

Discoverers of the Maya

No one outside the New World knew that the Maya existed until A.D. 1502. In that year, Christopher Columbus and some of his sailors spotted a Maya trading canoe in the Gulf of Honduras.

When other European explorers came to Central America, they made repeated contact with this vanishing civilization. For example, Francisco Córdoba, a Spanish soldier and explorer who discovered Yucatán in 1517, was the first Spaniard to find traces of the ancient Maya civilization. Seven years later Hernán Cortés and his party encountered the Maya as they crossed the central and southern Maya lowlands on a march from Mexico to Honduras. Cortés and his men were the first Europeans to pass through this region.

In search of riches and of empire, the Spaniards eventually conquered the Maya and claimed their land. The conquerors did not pause long to puzzle over the origin of the magnificent Maya cities that had been left to vanish beneath tropical growth. Apparently, they did not connect the living remnants they had conquered with the ruins they had seen. After the European invasion and conquest, the descendants of the ancient Maya all but disappeared. Time extinguished their traditions, and the jungle concealed their accomplishments.

Activities

KN
CO

1. Pretend that you are a sixteenth-century adventurer and ship's captain who has been commissioned to explore a part of Central America. Make a list of the supplies that you will need for your voyage. Be careful **not** to include any modern inventions.

CO
AP
SY

2. Pretend that, although you are a sixteenth-century adventurer, such recent inventions as refrigeration are inexplicably available to you. Taking their availability into account, draw up a revised list of supplies for the exploratory voyage described in activity 1. Then compare the two listings. In what ways are they similar? In what ways are they different? Under which conditions would travel have been easier? more convenient? more comfortable? What invention or inventions were most responsible for the differences between the two lists?

CO

3. Like the ancient Egyptians, the Maya wrote in hieroglyphs, small pictures that stood for words or ideas. Think of ten ideas that are most important to you and design hieroglyphs to represent these ideas.

CO
AP

4. The Maya used large oceangoing canoes to trade with their neighbors. Locate pictures and descriptions of these canoes. Then build a model of one.

Name_____

Rediscovery

Even though sixteenth-century Spanish explorers discovered the Maya, the world knew very little about them until they were rediscovered three hundred years later. In October 1839, John Lloyd Stephens, an American author-traveler, and Frederick Catherwood, a brilliant young English artist, went to Central America to search for the rumored ruins of a lost city. They sailed from New York to British Honduras (now called Belize), journeyed inland by river steamer to Lake Izabal in Guatemala, climbed the wall-like Sierra de las Minas, and then hacked their way through the uncharted rain forest which was purported to be holding an ancient city prisoner within its tangled branches.

At last their efforts were rewarded by the discovery of Copán, one of the southern centers of Maya civilization and a city of awe-inspiring monuments dedicated to unknown gods. Stephens dug, measured, and drew plans of the site while Catherwood painstakingly reproduced the hieroglyphs that he found on pyramid steps and on the tall stone columns called **stelae.** Stephens and Catherwood's well-documented report of their expedition focused the world's attention on Copán and on its builders—the Maya.

During the late nineteenth century, Alfred P. Maudslay, an English lord, carried out a thirteen-year systematic study of Maya sites. Journeying over wide areas of Central America, he carefully mapped and photographed many previously undiscovered ruins. In addition, he made plaster casts, sketches, and ink rubbings of Maya sculptures and hieroglyphs, and also collected pottery and other artifacts. His collection, which was housed in the British Museum, provided scholars who wished to study the Maya but were unable to travel to Central America with a wide variety of original material.

Activities

KN 1. On a globe or relief map of the world, trace a route John Lloyd Stephens and Frederick Catherwood might have followed from New York to Copán.

CO AP AN 2. Individual scientists often interpret archaeological finds in very different ways. They may have different theories about how and why buildings were constructed or about which tools were used at what times and in what ways. Select ten objects that represent your life. Tape a number to each object and place all of the objects in an empty shoe box or grocery sack. Take the box or sack to school. Ask five members of your class to be life-style experts, or scholars, and to identify each object, explain its significance, and then describe your life-style as it is represented by the ten objects. Ask these life-style scholars to make their observations and come to their conclusions without talking to one another and to write their notes and ideas on sheets of paper to share later.

SY 3. When all of the scholars have completed their study of your objects, compare their observations and conclusions. In what ways are they similar? In what ways are they different? Were the scholars helped in their interpretations by the fact that they know you and that their life-styles are similar to yours? Would the task have been more difficult if the scholars had been from an entirely different time and culture, if they had never met you, and if they had been forced to base their entire understanding of you on the ten objects?

EV 4. Evaluate the scholars' results. How accurate were their interpretations? Could you have supplied other objects that would have made their interpretations more accurate? How complete were their descriptions? How many more objects would the scholars have needed to make their descriptions complete?

Where Did the Maya Come From?

Once the Maya had been rediscovered, people became curious about this marvelous civilization. Who were the carvers of its stelae and the creators of its ruined cities, and where had they come from?

Archaeological evidence now suggests that the ancestors of the Maya traveled to Mesoamerica from Asia, a journey that took many generations and thousands of years. Twenty to forty thousand years ago, hunters and their families walked across a land bridge that once connected Russia with Alaska. Driven by their constant need for food and water, some of them gradually moved south, settling in the places we now know as Canada, the Pacific Northwest, California, the Southwest, and Mesoamerica.

Between 6000 and 2000 B.C., the people who had settled in Mesoamerica collected in small communities and began to grow plants for food. Among their crops were corn (or maize), squash, and beans. During the next two thousand years, some of these small communities grew large and powerful and developed their own political systems, religious beliefs, and forms of artistic expression—in short, their own distinct levels of cultural development, or civilizations.

The first of these distinctly Mesoamerican civilizations was that developed by the Olmecs between 1200 and 400 B.C. An enigmatic and energetic people, the Olmecs erected pyramid-mound ceremonial centers, carved massive stone statues and miniature jade figurines, depicted snarling jaguar deities in their art, and played a ritual ball game in which the players' movements symbolized the motions of the planets and stars. The Olmecs' written language, calendar system, and pantheon were very similar to those used, developed, and worshiped some years later by the Maya.

Though the precise beginnings of Maya civilization are difficult to pinpoint, there is no doubt that, by A.D. 250, the Maya had developed a culture that reflected the Olmec influence but was also distinct from that earlier form. Between 250 and 950, this culture flourished and spread throughout much of Mesoamerica. Then, within the next one hundred years, much of the vast Maya population vanished, leaving many of the Maya centers abandoned.

Activities

KN CO 1. Through battle, conquest, and trade, ancient Mesoamerican cultures came in contact with and influenced one another. Locate the names of some of these cultures. Use a time line or chart to show the dates of their dominance, and picture or describe some of their specific contributions to the Maya civilization and/or to the shared Mesoamerican culture.

KN CO 2. An **artifact** is a simple object, such as a tool or ornament, that has been made or modified by a human being. For example, a rock is not an artifact, but a rock that has been hollowed or rounded inward so that it will serve as a mortar for the grinding of corn or the crushing of spices is an artifact. List some of the artifacts a present-day archaeologist might expect to find at the site of an ancient village. List some of the artifacts a future archaeologist might find at the site of a twentieth-century town.

SY   Compare the lists. In what ways are they similar? In what ways are they different? Have human needs changed over the centuries? Or has the greatest change been in the ways human beings meet their needs?

EV   Evaluate these changes. Which ones represent real improvements in the overall human condition and which ones do not? For example, is a more varied diet necessarily more healthful or more nourishing? Are more accurate and more efficient weapons an improvement? Explain your answers.

Deciphering the Glyphs

Mesoamericans were the only ancient New World peoples to develop true writing systems. Examples of their writing can be found carved in stone monuments, painted on pottery and walls, and preserved in **codices,** folded manuscript books of bark paper or deerskin. While Mesoamerican writing varies according to time, culture, and language, all of it consists of pictures that stand for sounds, objects, or ideas.

The basic unit of the Maya system of writing is called a **glyph.** Usually, it is a group of pictures and symbols stylistically shaped to fill a square. Once John Lloyd Stephens and Frederick Catherwood had returned from Copán with copies of Maya glyphs, a major challenge facing scholars was to discover what meaning lay locked within these fantastic and sometimes grotesque shapes.

The Maya glyphs were difficult to decipher. There were more than eight hundred different ones, and many of them did not represent simple sounds or words. Instead they stood for important ideas or events. For example, there were specific Maya glyphs for birth, accession, capture, and burial.

Awed by time, the Maya tried to link their lives to its inevitable march, to tie history to astronomy by assigning each important event a position in their complex calendar. Thus, the Maya calendars became a key to both Maya history and the Maya language.

In fact, it was the Maya dating system that gave scholars the clue they needed to read the messages hidden in the glyphs. Among Maya manuscripts were some called the *Books of Chilam Balsam,* which had been written by Maya scribes in their own language using the Latin alphabet. When a scholar named D. G. Brinton translated these manuscripts late in the nineteenth century, he unraveled the Maya system of reckoning time and dating events, enabling scholars to read the fascinating stories of gods and rulers, cities and conquests, that had been painstakingly painted in the puzzling glyphs by Maya scribes many centuries before.

birth   accession   capture   burial

Activities

KN 1. Find pictures of some Maya glyphs and look at them.

CO
AP 2. Choose a Maya glyph that interests you. Copy it on a nine-inch-by-nine-inch piece of art paper. Draw it large enough to fill the paper. Using crayons or marking pens, color your glyph in earth tones. Display your glyph as part of a classroom "quilt." On a bulletin board or wall, mount your glyph side by side with those created by other members of your class to form a large square or rectangle. If you wish, pin or staple strips of rust or aqua construction paper between the glyphs and around their outside edge to serve as frames and a border.

CO
AP 3. Use a Maya glyph as the basis of the design for a stencil or simple block print. For example, you might make a Maya glyph potato print. Cut a potato in half. Using a pencil, draw some shapes from the glyph on one half of the potato. With a paring knife, cut away portions of the potato so that the glyph shapes are raised. Dip the potato in tempera paint or colored ink and print with it on white, eggshell, or tan paper. For an interesting effect, exchange potatoes with friends and create a printed design in which you use several different glyphs.

SY 4. Compare Maya glyphs with Egyptian hieroglyphs. In what ways are they similar? In what ways are they different? When making your comparison, consider both the style of the pictures, or symbols, and the things that they represent, or symbolize.

Time Marches On

The Maya feared time and were fascinated by the cosmic motions by which it is measured. They believed that time was a never-ending parade of gods who arbitrarily meted out doses of triumph and disaster. Ordinary people had no control over these gods, but priests might speak to them and divine the signs of good or bad fortune. To help their priests read and interpret these signs, the Maya used their considerable mathematical skill to develop at least three calendars, which they consulted before doing anything important.

The secrets of the Maya calendars were carefully guarded by the priests. Only they knew how to make and interpret the series of interrelated wheels, or disks, which were used to tell and record time. On the disks were carved or painted glyphs that represented the gods who were in charge of the days, months, years, and longer periods of time. The disks, which were set to turn independently, met to create combinations of glyphs that represented particular dates.

Each Maya calendar defined an endless passage of sunrises and sunsets since some selected base date. For example, in the Maya Long Count calendar, which was used most often, the base date, or beginning of time, was August 11, 3114 B.C. Under this system, the Maya year consisted of 365.242129 days. It was divided into eighteen months of twenty days each, with five days left over to be used at year's end for special religious ceremonies.

Activities

KN 1. Make a chart showing the names of some important Maya time cycles. Start with a day and end with 23,360,000,000 days.

KN CO 2. Do some research to learn about two other Maya calendars. What was each one called? What time periods did each one represent? For what special purpose was each one used?

CO AP 3. Look up the derivations of the names of our months. Develop a system of glyphs to represent these months and some of the holidays in them.

AP 4. Using cardboard, tagboard, or other stiff paper, create a system of interrelated disks to represent the major time increments of our calendar system (that is, the year, decade, century, and millenium). Show other class members how to use your disk calendar system.

Name_____

Maya Math

Math was very important to the Maya because it enabled them to make astronomical calculations and to devise an intricate calendric system by which they could regulate their physical and spiritual lives. Usually, however, only Maya priests knew how to make these vital calculations. Maya slaves, peasants, and nobles relied on priests to read and interpret the calendar. By means of these interpretations, the priests controlled all important aspects of Maya life, including government, religion, warfare, and trade.

In their mathematical notation, the Maya used only three symbols, or numerals:

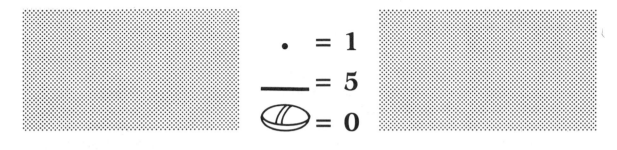

To write different numbers, the Maya combined these numerals in various ways. For example, in Maya numerals, the numbers 0 through 19 were written as follows:

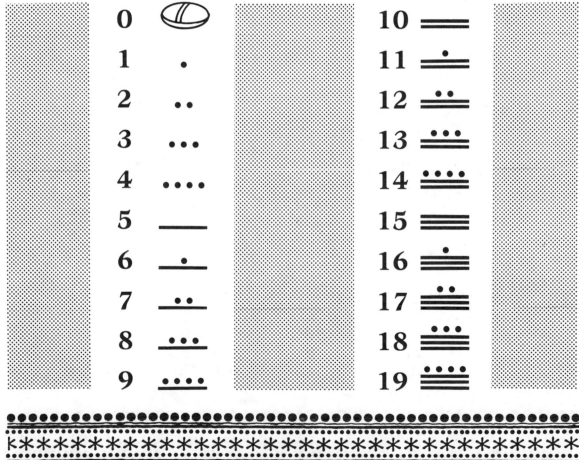

Maya Math
(continued)

In the Maya mathematical system, addition is easy. For example, if you are adding 5 (____) and 6 (__•__), you simply combine the numerals by stacking them vertically to give (▬▬), which is the Maya symbol for 11.

In problems 1 through 4, find the sums. Record your answers in both Maya and Arabic numerals.

1. • **+** __•__ =   =☐   3. •• **+** ▬▬ =   =☐

2. __•__ **+** __•__ =   =☐   4. ••• **+** ▬▬ =   =☐

To subtract one number from another, you remove the numerals that represent the smaller number from the numerals that represent the larger number. For example, if you are subtracting 6 (__•__) from 11 (▬▬), you remove, or erase, __•__ and are left with ____, which is the Maya symbol for 5.

In problems 5 through 8, find the remainders. Record your answers in both Arabic and Maya numerals.

5. ▬▬ **−** __•__ =   =☐   7. ••••▬▬ **−** ▬▬ =   =☐

6. ••••▬▬ **−** •••• =   =☐   8. ••••▬▬ **−** ••••▬▬ =   =☐

As you have probably noticed, the Maya mathematical system was based on increments of twenty, rather than on the increments of ten used in our decimal system. Another difference between the ancient Maya system and our modern one is that the Maya worked in vertical columns rather than in horizontal rows. For example, to increase by a power of ten, we move our notation one place, or column, to the left within a horizontal row. To increase by a power of twenty, the Maya moved their notation up one row within a vertical column.

Our Decimal System

10
100
1000
10000

The Maya System

1 •   20 ⬭   400 ⬭

Thus, in Maya numerals, the number 8,888 would be written as follows:

•	=	8000	(400 × 20)
••	=	800	(2 × 400)
••••	=	80	(4 × 20)
•••▬	=	8	(5 + 3)

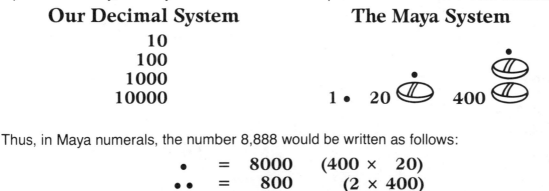

The Maya Pantheon

The Maya pantheon was very large because the Maya believed in many gods and goddesses. Most important among them were those connected with the Maya ideas about the creation of the universe. For example, the primary Maya deities were Hunab Ku, who created all life, and Hunab Ku's son Itzamna, who was god of the heavens. Itzamna had given man food, medicine, writing, and other wonderful gifts; and the Maya felt very close to him.

Also important to the Maya were the gods in charge of the layers of the universe. The Maya believed that the world had been made in a series of horizontal layers, thirteen in the upper world and nine in the lower world, the lowest of which was earth. According to Maya tradition, each layer had its own god. In addition, four gods—called the Bacabs—supported the four corners of the upper world, or heaven, a place of delights, free from suffering and labor.

Most of the Maya deities had dual personalities. For instance, Chac, the god of rain, sent the gentle showers needed to grow crops. If angered, however, he would send destructive floodwaters instead. The Maya made a continual effort to appeal to the pleasanter side of each deity's personality so that their lives would be free from tragedy and disaster. Prayers, offerings, and sacrifices filled their days. Priests became all-powerful because they were needed to interpret the gods' wishes and to conduct the intricate rituals that placated these fickle deities. Eventually, the Maya became weighed down by the complexity of their own religious beliefs and practices.

**Itzamna
god of the heavens**

**Chac
god of rain**

Activities

KN CO
1. Color was a very important element in Maya religion. Do some research to discover which colors were associated with which gods or events and why. Share your findings by means of a chart.

KN CO
2. Do some research to learn about one of the many ceremonies that the Maya conducted to placate their gods. Ask some friends to help you by demonstrating the ritual while you explain its significance to other members of your class.

KN CO AN SY
3. Make a chart on which you compare some members of the Maya pantheon with deities found in the Egyptian pantheon. Consider their attributes, their appearances, their hieroglyphic representations, their responsibilities, and their personalities. In what ways are they similar? In what ways are they different? Might some of the differences you have observed be reflections of the differences in the ancient Egyptian and Maya ways of life? Explain your answers.

How the Moon Came to Be

Long ago, there was a Maya chief who had a beautiful daughter. Because the chief loved his daughter very much and wanted her to stay with him always, he scared away all of her suitors, especially the sun, who was a very conceited fellow.

One day, while the chief was away in the jungle, the sun decided that he wanted to see the chief's daughter, so he sent one of his rays down to bring the girl up to him. The chief's daughter thought the sun handsome and returned his affection. Soon they were married.

When the Maya chief returned home and found his daughter gone, he was furious. He thought for days of only one thing—revenge. He asked the best blowgun maker in the land to make the largest, finest, and longest blowgun ever made.

Because the order was for a weapon so big and so fine, the gun maker set the entire village to work carving and sanding the gun and shaping the heavy balls of clay that would be shot through it. While the work continued, the Maya chief did exercises to strengthen his lungs: it would take tremendous power to blow just one of those heavy balls all the way to the sun!

Finally, the blowgun was finished, and the villagers carried it up to the top of a great hill. Standing triumphantly atop the hill, the Maya chief took a gigantic breath, summoned all of his strength, and blew into the gun with all his might. The villagers watched in admiration and terror as an enormous clay ball flew through the clear blue sky toward the bright face of the sun.

How the Moon Came to Be
(continued)

The Maya chief's strength was adequate, and his aim was accurate. The ball struck the sun; however, the ball had traveled so far, it had lost much of its momentum. The resulting blow did not hurt the sun, but it did startle him, causing him to drop the Maya chief's precious daughter. She tumbled from the sky into the ocean, where she broke into thousands of tiny pieces. Each piece wept pitifully and begged to be returned to the sun.

The little silvery fishes that lived in the ocean were much disturbed by the girl's weeping and felt very sorry for her. Gently, they collected her pieces and put them back together with scales from their own bodies. Although the fish did their best, the girl's shape was not the same as it had been before. She had an unforgettable face, but her supple frame and lithe limbs were gone.

Once the shattered girl had been mended, the little fishes collected beneath her and, in one united leap, lifted her back into the sky. Even though there were thousands of fishes, and each one of them leaped as high as it could, together they were not strong enough to reach the sun. Instead, they and the girl stuck to the nighttime sky.

And there they remain to this day. The silvery fishes can be seen as the Milky Way. As for the girl, she is now the moon and rides high in the heavens trying to catch the sun.

Activities

AP 1. Write a different ending for this myth.

AP
AN 2. What might have happened if the vengeful chief had been more successful in his efforts to punish the sun? Imagine that you are a villager who is trying to persuade the chief not to shoot at the sun because you fear the consequences of the sun's wrath. What would you say to persuade the chief? What terrible things might happen if he failed to listen to you?

AN
SY 3. Read another myth about the sun and the moon. Compare it with this Maya myth. In what ways are they similar? In what ways are they different?

Name _____

The Maya Look

The Maya took great pride in their appearance. Whether peasant or noble, they were carefully groomed and ornately decorated. The higher their social standing, the more elaborate their dress and ornamentation.

Peasant men wore very little, often only a woven loincloth, deerhide sandals, and a cloak knotted around their shoulders. Peasant women wore a slip and a sacklike garment of white cloth with holes cut for neck and arms. On their heads they wore long cotton scarves.

The best materials and fanciest designs were reserved for members of the upper classes. Dresses for women of noble rank were made of beautifully woven cotton and decorated with brilliantly dyed embroidery. In addition, these women often wore stoles of bright color and complicated design. Men of noble rank wore loincloths that were magnificently decorated with feathers, jaguar skin, and embroidery. Their cloaks were made from fine materials woven in extremely complex patterns.

The most elaborate of all Maya attire were the headdresses worn by the nobles of highest rank. The long, irridescent tail feathers of the quetzal, a rare bird, were used in these headdresses, which were built to great heights on wooden frames. Sometimes the headdresses were taller than the men who wore them!

Completing the Maya look were fancy jewelry, complicated hairstyles, and painted bodies. Jewelry and other similar ornaments were loved by all. Maya ears, noses, lips, knees, necks, wrists, and ankles were seldom without decoration of some kind. Both men and women wore their hair long, braided in two or four braids, and fixed in a variety of complex arrangements. The Maya painted their bodies in colors set by tradition. Warriors wore red and black, priests wore blue, teenagers wore black, and prisoners were striped in black and white.

The Maya Look
(continued)

Activities

KN 1. Quetzals were highly prized by the Maya and were represented in many places and ways in the Maya world. Look at pictures of Maya architecture and artifacts. Make a list of the places and ways in which you find the quetzal's name or symbol used.

KN CO 2. First, read about Maya feathercraft, sandal making, and weaving. Then, select one of these crafts and create an illustrated step-by-step chart to show how it was practiced by the Maya.

KN AP 3. Study illustrations of Maya nobles' head-dresses. Then draw a picture of a headdress you would like to wear to an important festival.

KN CO AP 4. You have been hired to create a mail-order catalog for a firm specializing in Maya clothing. It is your job both to draw the pictures and to write the text. Make the pictures colorful and make all of the descriptions so exciting that people will rush to buy the clothing, jewelry, and headdresses they need to give them the Maya look.

What Price Beauty!

For a Maya, the road to beauty was paved with pain. The Maya had definite ideas about appearance, and they were willing to remodel their bodies to make them conform to these ideas. For example, the Maya squeezed their babies' heads between two boards. The constant pressure gradually pushed the forehead back at a slant, elongating the head and making it rise to a point.

Because the Maya liked crossed eyes, mothers would tie beads or balls of wax to their children's hair so that these beads or balls dangled between their eyes. The children would turn their eyes in to look at the swinging pendants so often and so much that their eyes would become crossed and remain so.

Maya remodeling was not limited to babies and children. In fact, the painful process continued even after the Maya reached adulthood. Men burned bald spots on the tops of their heads. They also filed their teeth to sharp points or covered them with plates of precious stone. Both men and women tattooed their faces and bodies in complicated designs, which were cut into their skin. The tattooing process was so painful that the Maya were often sick for days afterward.

What Price Beauty!
(continued)

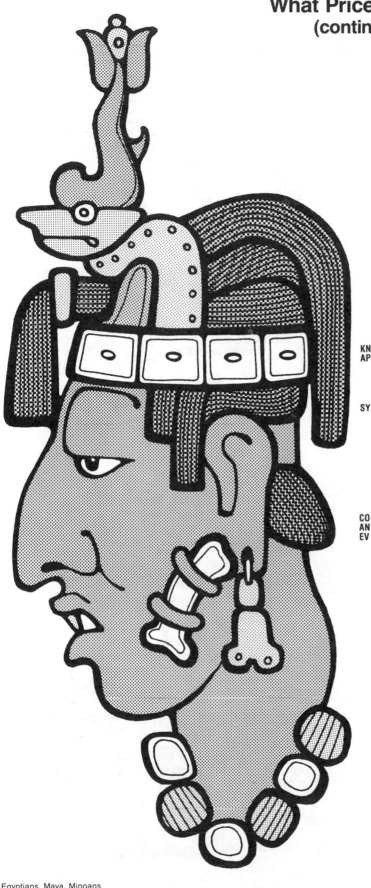

For Maya nobles, all of these processes were exaggerated. For example, the heads of nobles were shaped to a steeper slant and sharper point. At times, their noses were broken and reset to make them "high bridged"—what we call hooked—a look that the Maya very much admired. Huge holes were poked in their ears, lips, and noses so that heavy ornaments could be hung from them. Designs were cut into their teeth, and jade was inlaid in the designs. In what must be one of the earliest known examples of plastic surgery, Maya nobles even had less attractive parts of their bodies cut and reshaped into more fashionable form.

Activities

KN AP 1. Make a poster advertising services that might have been performed in a Maya beauty or barber shop.

SY 2. Look at beauty shop advertisements in your local newspaper. Make a list of the services offered by these shops. Compare present-day beauty practices with ancient Maya ones. In what ways are they similar? In what ways are they different?

CO AN EV 3. Many things that the Maya did more than one thousand years ago to make themselves attractive seem strange to us today. List some things that people do today to make themselves attractive. Which of these things might seem strange—or even bizarre—to someone reading about them more than one thousand years from now?

Ceramic Splendor

The Maya were expert artisans. Working without a potter's wheel, Maya women produced ceramic work of remarkable beauty and craftsmanship. Pottery dating back further than 2000 B.C. has been found at identified Maya sites, but Maya pottery making reached its zenith between 550 A.D. and 800 A.D., the period in Maya history that is termed Late Classic. During this time, the Maya perfected polychrome painting; and the pottery of this period is characterized by a more varied use of color—rich reds, vibrant oranges, warm browns, soft creams, and shiny blacks—a stronger sense of design, and a more expressive line than the pottery created in earlier periods.

The Maya used pottery bowls, jars, and other vessels in many ways—to collect and store water, to prepare and serve food, to record and commemorate important events, to burn incense, and to represent and honor their deities. On these clay pieces, Maya artisans depicted animals, people, and gods. Sometimes, they painted portraits of famous chiefs or pictures of important events. In addition, the Maya created figurines and other pottery pieces that were purely decorative. Apparently, the Maya took pleasure in both creating and admiring their ceramic splendor.

Activities

KN 1. The first sentence on this page states that "the Maya were expert artisans." Discover the difference between an **artist** and an **artisan.**

EV 2. Look at pictures or actual examples of Maya portrait vases painted during the Late Classic period. Evaluate these ceramic pieces to decide whether the Maya women who made them were artisans or artists. Justify your decision.

Name_____

Ceramic Splendor Activity Sheet

KN
CO
AP
You are a Maya potter of recognized skill. Word of your reputation has reached the ears of an exalted Maya ruler. He has carefully examined examples of your work and has chosen you for a special project. He has commissioned you to create a pottery bowl, column, figurine, or vase depicting the most important event in his life. On the line below, name or describe this event. Then, in the space provided, sketch an outline of the pottery piece you intend to create. Using the Maya palette—rich reds, vibrant oranges, warm browns, soft creams, and shiny blacks—add the pictures and designs with which you plan to decorate the piece so that the Maya ruler can approve these details before you begin.

Event: _____

So Much with So Little

The Maya were a Stone Age people who developed a surprisingly sophisticated civilization characterized by remarkable achievements in mathematics, calendrics, architecture, and art. Without wheels, they erected monumental stone structures and created exquisite pottery pieces. Without metal tools, they painstakingly chipped and scratched intricate patterns and pictures into every available surface.

The amazing thing about Maya artists is that they were able to produce so much with so little. Relying only on crude tools and their unique aesthetic vision, Maya sculptors created superb stone monuments, architectural embellishments, jade ornaments, elaborate thrones, and decorative figurines.

With hammers and chisels, Maya sculptors chipped away at many different kinds of stone. Their free-standing monuments, called **stelae,** were usually made from limestone or obsidian monoliths. City buildings and temples were often built from sandstone or limestone blocks. And fancy figurines were carved from jade, a material that was viewed as a symbol of status and was highly prized.

Just as the designs painted on early Maya pottery were less intricate and lifelike than those painted on the polychromatic pottery of the Classic period, so early Maya sculpture tended to be flatter and less realistic than later works. Sculptures of the Classic period depicted rulers, gods, ceremonies, battles, and processions in powerful, rounded images that mixed reality and symbolism.

Activities

KN CO 1. The first sentence on this page states that the Maya "were a Stone Age people." Do some research to discover what criteria archaeologists and anthropologists use to classify a culture as belonging to the Stone Age and to learn the names, dates, and locations of other recognized Stone Age cultures.

KN CO 2. You are an archaeologist. You find a funeral mask in a Maya tomb. List the features of the mask which might indicate that it was created for an exalted ruler. Draw a picture of the mask or make a funeral mask from papier-mâché.

KN CO 3. Investigate the stone Chac Mool sculptures. Where were they found? What do they represent? What influenced their design? What was their purpose? What is their significance?

KN CO AP 4. You are a skilled Maya sculptor. Write a résumé to submit to civic leaders so that they will consider you for a commission to decorate some city buildings. Be sure to present a brief statement of your artistic philosophy, describe your education and training, and include an annotated list of your best and/or most impressive works. You may also wish to enclose sketches of some of your most important pieces.

Name_____

So Much with So Little Activity Sheet

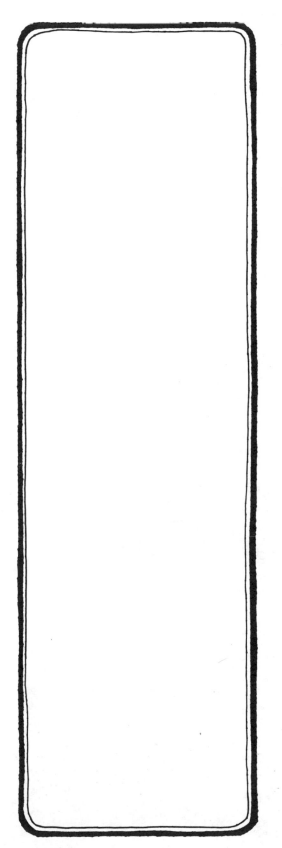

KN
CO
AP

A **stela** is a carved or inscribed stone pillar used for commemorative purposes. Throughout history, stelae have been erected to mark the sites of important events and the graves of important people. The Maya were no exception to this custom. They carved ornate stelae from huge pieces of limestone and obsidian, often covering the entire rock surface with intricate designs, glyphs, and pictures. They used stelae to record history and mark the passing of time.

Decorate this stela to commemorate some important events in your life. Use Maya-style designs, glyphs, and/or pictures. Beside each one, write what it means or commemorates.

Just for Fun

AN
SY

Compare the **totem poles** made by the Algonquians in North America with the stelae carved by the Maya in Mesoamerica. In what ways are they similar? In what ways are they different? In making your comparison, consider the material from which each was made, the style in which each was decorated, and the specific use to which each was put.

Name_____

Gems in the Ancient World

Architecture was one of the chief expressions of Maya genius. What became a Maya construction boom began around A.D. 250. For the next 650 years, Maya architect-priests created buildings of great beauty and huge size. They erected large religious centers throughout the Maya area of Mesoamerica. With additions over the years, these religious centers became majestic cities that sparkled like gems in the ancient world.

Maya architects liked to place their buildings on high ground. For construction sites, they chose the hills whose tops rose above the surrounding rain forest and altered them to suit their needs. For example, before erecting a city, they laid a single, gigantic platform. These platforms were made of carefully fitted stones and were sometimes many miles square. They served as foundations for the elaborate ceremonial centers that were erected upon them.

Each ceremonial center contained several temples. The temples designed by Maya architect-priests were magnificent structures. Built on high platforms in stacks of rectangles of decreasing size, much like many-layered wedding cakes, they were sometimes as high as ten or fifteen stories. Wide stairways with hundreds of shallow steps led up each side to a small room at the top, which was used for religious ceremonies. Atop this room was a carved roof crest that resembled a rooster's comb and is sometimes called the roof comb.

Gems in the Ancient World
(continued)

Because Maya buildings consisted of solid stacks of stone with few openings, they had massive exteriors. To prevent their buildings from looking too heavy, the Maya covered each one with a gleaming coat of white or cream-colored plaster, into which they carved beautiful scenes and on which they painted in bright colors.

When it was time for remodeling and urban renewal, the Maya did not tear down the old and replace it with the new. Instead, they erected new and larger buildings directly over and around the smaller, older ones. In this way, the old became a tiny, interior part of the new. This practice has made it possible for archaeologists who excavate Maya temples to see layer after layer of older and older architecture that has been carefully protected from the ravages of time and weather.

Activities

KN CO AP

1. First, study pictures and diagrams of Maya temples. Then, construct a model of one using papier-mâché, styrofoam blocks, sugar cubes, or some other similar building material.

KN CO AP

2. Two of the materials from which the Maya constructed their temples were limestone and sandstone. Both of these rocks are classified as **sedimentary,** which means that they were formed from fragments carried from their source and deposited by water. Do some research to learn about the geologic history and characteristics of that part of Mesoamerica which was inhabited by the ancient Maya. Where are the large deposits of limestone and sandstone found? How did they get there? How far are they from the sites of Maya temples?

KN CO AP

3. In building their temples, did the Maya use stones they found at the site or did they quarry and transport blocks of stone over long distances? The Maya did not have metal tools or wheels to aid them in their construction projects. Experiment to discover what simple mechanical devices the Maya might have used to help them move heavy rocks from place to place.

KN CO AP AN

4. Archaeologists are curious about why the Maya, who lived primarily in lowland rain forests, built many of their temples on hilltops. One theory suggests that the reason was the need for communication among Maya centers. According to this theory, the temples may have been arranged to permit line-of-sight communication between them and, thus, between the Maya population centers they served. Such communication might have been by means of flags, smoke signals, or flashes of light. With a friend, experiment with one of these communication methods. For example, you might use mirrors and Morse code to send messages by means of long and short flashes of sunlight.

KN CO AP AN

5. Do some research to learn more about nonelectronic means of communication. How many different ways can you think of for members of a Stone Age culture to send and receive messages? Remember that much of the Maya writing was on stone and would have been difficult to carry from place to place.

A Visit to Tikal

Travel back in time to A.D. 800 to the bustling metropolis of Tikal, Guatemala, where the Maya have lived since 600 B.C. Largest of the Maya cities, Tikal covers about forty-six square miles and is protected by a wall and a moat. It contains at least three thousand buildings, eight of which are enormous temple-pyramids, and houses about forty thousand people.

The city is spacious and immaculate. Tall buildings are placed far apart so that each one can be easily seen and individually admired. All buildings are covered with white or cream-colored plaster, and their external walls are alive with bright paintings and intricate carvings.

A wide, stone-paved road leads to the Great Plaza, a carefully leveled platform in the center of the city. The Great Plaza lies between two large, man-made reservoirs, built to store water for the city. The walls of these reservoirs also serve as roads, or **causeways.**

Straight out one wide causeway you see the tallest of all Maya temples. It is more than 230 feet high and is terraced so that it resembles a multilayered, rectangular wedding cake. Hundreds of shallow steps ascend each of its four sides.

Before your eyes, the people of Tikal go about their daily tasks. Women weave threads into cloth and form moist clay into bowls and jars. Men move and lay stones to erect new buildings and to enlarge and improve old ones. They also plant and tend fields of corn, beans, and squash. As you look at the bustling life before you, it is hard to believe that this city did not exist at all two thousand years ago and that all of it will be abandoned in less than two hundred years.

A Visit to Tikal
(continued)

Activities

KN
CO

1. First, acquaint yourself with several Maya sites and cities. Then, pretend that you are a travel agent. Among your clients are an astronomer, a cryptologist, a hieroglyphics expert, and a librarian. Write a note to each of these clients recommending a Maya city he or she might especially enjoy visiting and explaining the reasons for your recommendations.

KN
CO
AP

2. You are a traveling column salesperson. You carry a full line of the very best Greek and Egyptian columns and are trying to persuade the Maya to buy and use some of them. What would be your sales pitch? Create an illustrated brochure or other sales piece to make your task easier.

AP
AN

3. Knowing what you know about the Maya mind and Maya standards of beauty, which of your columns do you think they will prefer? Why?

Name_____

The Secret of Palenque

The elegant white buildings of Palenque in Chiapas, Mexico, sit on a ledge of green hill below a forested highland. The architecture of this ancient city fits the shape of the land, and it is considered to be one of the most beautiful Maya centers. Until rather recently, Palenque's superficial beauty concealed an astounding secret. Locked deep inside a towering temple was something that had escaped discovery despite years of exploration and study within that very building—the secret of Palenque.

In 1945, archaeologist Alberto Ruz Lhuillier was studying the Temple of Inscriptions, which stands atop a seventy-foot-high pyramid in Palenque. In the course of his studies, he noticed some unusual things about the temple's interior. For example, the inner walls continued below the level of the floor. In addition, the floor was made of carefully fitted stones. Three holes had been drilled in one of these stones, and the holes had then been partly concealed with stone plugs. The relative positions of the holes caused Ruz to speculate that they might be finger holes, once used for lifting the stone. If that was so, the archaeologist reasoned, there must be something of interest below the temple floor.

Ruz had the stone plugs removed. Then, using the holes as grips, he raised the heavy floor stone. Beneath it lay a stairway filled with dirt and debris. It took three years to clear the stairway and to discover that it led far below to the core of the pyramid. Then more digging revealed a large burial vault containing the skeletons of six young men, apparently victims of the common Maya practice of human sacrifice.

Ruz's explorations did not stop at that vault. Ruz reasoned that the Maya would not have gone to so much trouble just to bury six sacrificial victims. Certain that the pyramid held a deeper mystery, he and his men continued to work.

After several more days, Ruz and his men were able to remove a gigantic, triangular stone that blocked their passage. Behind that stone lay another chamber. Around its walls in stucco relief were the nine Maya Lords of the Underworld. Within the chamber was a great stone slab thirteen feet long. On the surface of this slab was carved a picture of a man resting on a throne. Around the man were symbols and calendric hieroglyphics which indicated that the mysterious chamber was actually the tomb of Pacal the Great, who governed the prosperous city of Palenque during most of the seventh century A.D.

In 1952, Alberto Ruz Lhuillier had discovered the secret of Palenque. He had found the only known pyramid tomb in the Americas and had become the first person to enter this tomb in more than one thousand years.

Activities

KN CO AP

1. Earl H. Morris made another spectacular discovery at Palenque. Find out what it was and write a short play about it.

KN CO SY EV

2. First, draw floor plans and diagrams of the exteriors and interiors of the tomb pyramid at Palenque and of an Egyptian tomb pyramid. Then, compare them. In what ways are they similar? In what ways are they different? Which pyramid is more technologically advanced in its construction? Which pyramid is more beautiful? Explain your responses.

Name_____

"Painted Walls"

How would you like to discover something that immeasurably advanced the world's knowledge of a vanished civilization? In 1946, Giles G. Healy made this kind of discovery. Healy, an explorer and photographer, had gone to Chiapas, Mexico, to film a documentary about the Lacondon Indians, remnants of the Maya. While there, he observed that the men of the tribe left periodically to go to a secret shrine somewhere in the dense jungle. His curiosity aroused, Healy persuaded some of the men to take him with them on their next pilgrimage.

What Healy discovered was extraordinary. In the jungle was a lost city. Within the city was a raised citadel. Atop this citadel was a three-roomed temple overgrown with vines but surprisingly well preserved. And on the interior walls of this temple were exquisite murals depicting all aspects of Maya life. In brilliant color and fine detail, these wall paintings showed priests in processions, warriors in battle, and dancers in costume; but they also showed the Maya in less formal moments engaged in less important pursuits. Archaeologists have determined that the murals were painted between A.D. 400 and A.D. 900. Together, they are a picture encyclopedia of Maya life and customs during this period.

The hidden city Healy visited was christened Bonampak, a Mayan word meaning "painted walls," in honor of the murals Healy found.

Activities

1. Select and cut from magazines pictures that will give people living one thousand years from now an accurate impression of our life and customs. Use these pictures to create a large montage.

2. Think of scenes that would give people living one thousand years from now an accurate picture of our life and customs and draw them as part of a large classroom mural.

3. If only a few photographs or paintings could be preserved from this century for future archaeologists to find and use to understand and interpret our culture, which ones would give them the most accurate picture? Why?

A Complex Social Structure

The Maya had a complex social structure divided into four main levels and many sub-levels. On the highest social level were the priests. They controlled government, religion, warfare, and trade. The high priest was the supreme authority over a city and its outlying areas. The priests were supported entirely by the peasants, who paid huge tributes and gave free labor.

The next level was the nobility. Members of this group were a privileged class. They paid no taxes, and jobs of any importance were given to them. Civil servants, military officers, merchants, craftsmen, and architects for city buildings were chosen from their ranks.

Members of these privileged classes—the priests and nobility—lived in the larger Maya cities, while the peasants lived in small villages and in the countryside. The villages were governed by priest-rulers, who often treated themselves to luxurious houses, furs, and servants, had many assistants, and kept themselves widely separated from their subjects.

The next level within Maya society was occupied by the peasants. They worked hard and paid huge tributes to the elite. They were not allowed to get an education or to own objects, such as quetzal feathers and jade, that were signs of status. Members of this group often became the hapless victims when the priests decided that human sacrifice was needed to calm the gods.

Name_____

A Complex Social Structure
(continued)

The lowest level within the Maya social structure was occupied by the slaves. This group included orphans, criminals, prisoners of war and other captured enemy, and the children of slaves. Slaves were not mistreated; but they did almost all of the hard manual labor necessary to construct Maya cities and to keep them functioning, and they had no privileges. It was to the slaves that priests looked first in search of victims for human sacrifice.

Activities

KN CO AP 1. You are a Maya monarch in need of servants. Write an advertisement detailing the kinds of servants that you need and the special qualifications you will expect each one to have. Also mention the benefits that await any qualified applicants.

KN CO AP 2. You are a *halach uinic.* Find out what that is and then write a letter describing your house, your duties, and your way of life.

Pok-a-Tok

As long ago as the sixth century B.C., the Maya played pok-a-tok, a sacred ball game whose primary purpose was to win favor with the gods. The exact rules of the game are not known, but it was fast paced and included elements of racquet ball, soccer, basketball, and volleyball.

Like racquet ball, pok-a-tok was played with a bouncy rubber ball on a walled court, but there was no racquet. Instead, pok-a-tok players hit the ball with parts of their bodies. As in soccer, pok-a-tok players were not permitted to hold or throw the ball with their hands; however, they were allowed to strike it with their fists, elbows, and seats and, in this way, to direct it toward a ring attached to the middle of a wall.

Sending a ball through a ring, or hoop, sounds like basketball, but this ring was oriented vertically, rather than horizontally, and was twenty to thirty feet above the ground, instead of ten. In addition, the ring opening was barely wide enough to accommodate the six-inch diameter of the ball. Scoring must have been nearly impossible.

In pok-a-tok, while the primary object of the game was to score by putting the ball through the ring, the secondary object was to keep the ball in motion for as long as possible. As in volleyball, spectators enjoyed watching the players try to keep the ball in the air by hitting it. Pok-a-tok players were not allowed to take time out from the action or to enjoy the luxury of quarter or halftime breaks. Instead, they played continuously until the game was over. As you might imagine, during long, grueling games, heat, humidity, and fatigue frequently took their toll, causing even the most athletic players to collapse from exhaustion.

Name_____

Pok-a-Tok
(continued)

The Maya took their pok-a-tok games seriously. Only professional athletes were allowed to play, and they were coached by priests. Good pok-a-tok players were very popular, and winners were generously rewarded. Their pictures were painted on pottery and walls; and when a player scored, he was permitted to claim the clothing and jewelry of any spectators he could catch.

Losers did not fare so well. Because the Maya thought that their unsuccessful performance might have angered watching deities, these hapless athletes were often sacrificed to appease the gods.

Activities

KN
CO
AP

1. Pok-a-tok players were completely outfitted with special uniforms and equipment. Not only did they wear decorative clothing and helmets, but they also donned leather gloves, elbow pads, knee pads, and hip pads. You have been commissioned to design uniforms for a pok-a-tok team known as the Copán Jaguars. First, create an emblem to go with this name. Then, draw sketches to show how you would use this emblem on a helmet, a T-shirt or jersey, and a pennant.

KN
CO
AP

2. You are a media sports commentator covering the Mesoamerican Championship Pok-a-Tok Playoffs. Write a broadcast script that includes pregame introductions, play-by-play commentary, and a postgame wrap-up for this all-important series.

The Maya Mystery

"It is impossible to describe the interest with which I explored these ruins. ...The beauty of the sculptures, the solemn stillness of the woods disturbed only by the screaming of the monkeys and the chattering of the parrots, the desolation of the city, and the mystery that hung over it, created an interest higher, if possible, than I had ever felt among the ruins of the Old World," wrote John Lloyd Stephens about his explorations of the ruined Maya city of Copán in Honduras. "All was mystery," he continued, "dark, impenetrable mystery." And much of it is still mystery, despite the fact that scholars have spent more than one hundred years attempting to solve the mystery by explaining what happened to the Maya.

The Maya were creators of a great civilization. In the areas of architecture, art, astronomy, and mathematics, they achieved unparalleled levels of excellence. They built magnificent cities, equal in size and complexity to many of our own. Then suddenly, between A.D. 850 and 900, everything just stopped, and the magnificent cities were abandoned.

Since the discovery of these abandoned cities more than one hundred years ago, scholars and archaeologists have advanced theory after theory in their futile attempts to explain what happened to the Maya. Perhaps they were victims of a sudden, catastrophic change in climate or of a natural disaster, such as an earthquake, volcanic eruption, fire, or flood. Maybe their cities were invaded and pillaged by a more warlike tribe. Or perhaps a disease the Maya could not cure became an epidemic they could not stop. Thus far, the evidence has not supported any one of these theories exclusively.

The Maya Mystery
(continued)

One theory is gaining popularity among scholars, and no evidence has yet been found to disprove it. This theory suggests that social unrest, or revolution, may have ended centuries of Maya development. According to this theory, the peasants tired of paying huge tributes to the priests and rulers, and of providing endless hours of hard labor to support an affluent life-style they were not permitted to share. They rebelled against this life-style, killing members of the ruling classes, and then returned to their meager farms in the countryside, leaving the magnificent cities to be reclaimed by the sur-rounding rain forest.

Activities

KN
CO
AP
AN
1. The violent eruption of Mount Vesuvius in A.D. 79 brought an abrupt end to life in the ancient port city of Pompeii, near Naples, Italy. First, read about this disaster. Then, write an essay in which you explain what geologic and archaeological evidence would be needed to support the theory that a widespread volcanic eruption ended Maya civilization.

AN
2. Imagine that all of the people in New York, Chicago, Dallas, or San Francisco abandoned that city without leaving behind any indication of where they had gone or why they had left. Why might people suddenly abandon a city? List all of the reasons you can think of.

AN
SY
EV
3. As head of an archaeological committee, you must evaluate scholars' theories about the disap-pearance of the Maya. First, read about several of the theories mentioned above. Then, create a table or chart in which you list the theories, summarize them, and briefly describe the evidence that supports or refutes each one. Finally, indicate which theory you believe to be valid and why.

Correlated Activities

AP With a small group or your entire class, pretend that you have a spoken language but no writing system and wish to develop one. Decide what words or concepts most need to be represented and develop recognizable symbols to stand for them. Your writing system may consist of letters, glyphs, or a combination of both of these, but it should be consistent so that it can be easily learned and used.

KN CO SY The English word **calendar** comes from the Latin word **Kalendae,** the name given to the first day of each Roman month and a word generalized in some Latin contexts to mean "month." Thus, a calendar is a collection of months or, less specifically, a system of reckoning time.

In devising such systems, people have usually relied on the recurrent cycles they observe in nature—the cycles of the sun and of the moon. For example, they have established a year of solar seasons and divided it into lunar months. The problem is that lunar and solar months are not equal in length. Attempts throughout history to harmonize solar and lunar timekeeping have produced a series of calendars.

Do some research to learn about the ancient calendars developed in Mesopotamia and in Egypt. Also acquaint yourself with the Roman, Julian, Gregorian, Jewish, and Aztec calendars. Select two of these calendars and compare them. In what ways are they similar? In what ways are they different? Which ones are solar? Which ones are lunar? Which ones are combinations? Which ones are most accurate? Which one of the calendars in use today is the only widely used purely lunar calendar?

KN CO SY Explore the relationships among color, religious belief, and social status in Maya culture. Then compare these relationships with similar relationships in some modern culture. For example, consider how the Maya felt about blue. What might have happened if a blue-skinned giant had appeared among them? Until quite recently, what colors were the stripes on the uniforms worn by convicts in United States prisons? In what colors did the Maya stripe their prisoners?

AP SY First, create a series of time lines representing the rise, major achievements, and fall of several ancient civilizations. Then compare these time lines and the civilizations they represent with regard to duration, the sequence of achievements, and the probable causes of decline and disappearance.

AP AN SY The Maya played a game using a ball and devised a calendrical system using three interrelated disks. Obviously, they were aware of round objects—both spheres and circles—yet, so far as we know, they made no practical use of the wheel. Why? Offer either a scientific theory or a mythological explanation of the Maya's apparent failure to apply the wheel in their daily lives.

AN SY EV First, with a small group or your entire class, brainstorm reasons for the Maya's disappearance. Next, select one or two of the most plausible reasons and propose them in more detail as theories. Then, do some research to learn what existing archaeological evidence reveals about the Maya's mysterious disappearance. Finally, evaluate your theories in light of this evidence and select the one that seems most valid.

Correlated Activities
(continued)

You are the curator of a natural history museum. It is your job to organize an exhibit to give museum visitors some understanding of the Maya.

KN CO AP Describe the setting you will create for the exhibit. Consider how you will make the exhibit appeal to all five senses—sight, hearing, taste, smell, and touch. For example, might you use plants? Might you include music and serve food? If so, which plants, musical compositions, and dishes will you use and why?

KN CO Select and list the kinds of artifacts and objects you will include in the exhibit. Rely on your own knowledge of what is available and on your own feelings about what people would like to see. Consider everyday objects as well as fancier and more formal things.

CO Choose five of the artifacts and objects you have listed and explain in detail how you will display each one. Will it be placed high, at eye level, or low? Will it be in a protective case where it can only be looked at or out in the open where it can be touched and felt?

AP Choose a name for the exhibit and create a logogram or symbol for it.

AP Design a brochure, flier, or poster to interest people in coming to see the exhibit. Explain in a few words the purpose and content of the exhibit, when and where it will be on display, the price (if any) that will be charged for admission, and how groups can make arrangements to view it.

AP Create a program for the exhibit. In the program, provide an introduction in which you give museum visitors some background information about Maya history and culture. Also, picture and describe each of the artifacts and objects you have selected for the exhibit and explain its historical or cultural significance.

AP Design T-shirts, tote bags, badges, or other similar items for sale to exhibit visitors in the museum souvenir and gift shop.

Name_____

Posttest

Circle the letter beside the best answer or the most appropriate response.

1. The Maya are classified by anthropologists as a Stone Age people because of
   a. the rocky land they farmed.
   b. the stone statues they carved.
   c. the temples they constructed.
   d. the tools they used.

2. **Stelae** are
   a. clusters of stars.
   b. headdresses worn by Maya nobles.
   c. inscribed stone pillars.
   d. equipment used by athletes.

3. An **artifact** is
   a. an authentic work of art.
   b. a statement that has been or can be proved to be true.
   c. something that is artificial.
   d. a simple object made or modified by a human being.

4. A **codex** is
   a. the code used by the Maya for important wartime messages.
   b. an ancient, handwritten record, often of historical or religious significance.
   c. a special ornament placed atop all Maya temples.
   d. the animal most admired by the Maya.

5. A **causeway** is
   a. a raised highway, especially one built across wet ground or over water.
   b. a highway built for a particular reason or special purpose.
   c. the steep stairway up the side of a Maya temple-pyramid.
   d. the secret passageway within a Maya temple-pyramid.

6. At Palenque, Alberto Ruz Lhuillier discovered
   a. an assortment of sophisticated stone tools.
   b. a temple protected by sphinxes.
   c. the only known pyramid tomb in the Americas.
   d. wheels used by Maya construction crews.

7. The Maya word **bonampak** means
   a. "lost city."
   b. "brave warrior."
   c. "tall temple."
   d. "painted walls."

8. Maya athletes played a sacred ball game called
   a. quetzal.
   b. senet.
   c. pok-a-tok.
   d. Ouija.

9. In the stratified Maya social structure, which group controlled government, religion, warfare, and trade?
   a. priests
   b. nobles
   c. peasants
   d. slaves

10. Scholars now suggest that Maya civilization ended abruptly because of
    a. a tidal wave.
    b. a volcanic eruption.
    c. an atomic explosion.
    d. social unrest, or revolution.

Answer Key

Pretest, Page 36		Posttest, Page 70	
1. c	6. a	1. d	6. c
2. a	7. b	2. c	7. d
3. b	8. d	3. d	8. c
4. c	9. a	4. b	9. a
5. d	10. c	5. a	10. d

This is to certify that

____

(name of student)

has satisfactorily completed a unit of study on the

Maya

and has been named a

Master of Mesoamericana

in recognition of this accomplishment.

____

(signature of teacher)

____

(date)

Minoans

Bulletin Board Ideas

THE WORD WORKS

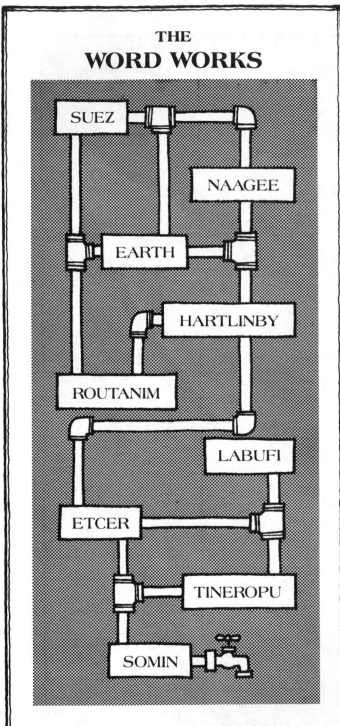

SUEZ

NAAGEE

EARTH

HARTLINBY

ROUTANIM

LABUFI

ETCER

TINEROPU

SOMIN

Unscramble these words. Write the correct spelling for each word on a piece of paper. Beside it write a definition and a brief explanation of its association with the Minoans or its importance to them.

CRETAN TIME LINE

6000 B.C.	Primitive farmers settle on the northern shore.
3000 B.C.	Settlers from western Asia bring Stone Age culture.
3000–2200 B.C.	**Early Minoan Age**
2200–1600 B.C.	**Middle Minoan Age**
1600 B.C.	Cretan kingdom reaches its greatest power, prosperity, and civilization.
1600–1200 B.C.	**Late Minoan Age**
1470 B.C.	Thera is wracked by an earthquake and volcanic eruption.
1450 B.C.	All Minoan palaces, except the one at Knossos, have been destroyed, perhaps by Mycenaeans.
A.D. 1893	Sir Arthur Evans begins excavating at Knossos.

Learning Center Idea

KNOSSOS KNOWLEDGE

The grandest of all the palaces on the island of Crete was the palace at Knossos. To increase your knowledge of this palace, take part in a research dig. Start at the top and uncover interesting information by completing each project.

Sir Arthur Evans spent more than forty years excavating and reconstructing the palace at Knossos and studying its builders, the Minoans. Find five additional facts about this British archaeologist.

King Minos lived in this palace with his wife Pasiphae. According to myth, the Minotaur was Poseidon's way of punishing Minos. Who was Poseidon? Why was he angry with the Cretan king? What did the Minotaur look like?

The palace at Knossos was built in wings around an open courtyard. On the north were extensive workshops for use by the king's artists and craftsmen. Do research to learn what materials these artists and craftsmen used. Then draw pictures to show some of the objects they made.

On the east were the royal apartments. Read a description of these apartments, imagine how they might have looked, and draw a picture of them.

The Minoans are credited with being way ahead of their time because of their invention and use of indoor plumbing. Find out how Minoan plumbing worked and how modern plumbing works. Use labeled diagrams to compare these two systems.

The Minoans made extensive use of **light wells** in their buildings. Draw a picture of a light well and describe the advantages and disadvantages of incorporating this feature in a house or palace.

According to myth, a **labyrinth** was built in the basement of the palace at Knossos to confine the Minotaur. Draw a maze, or labyrinth, on a piece of paper. When your drawing is finished, challenge a friend to start in the center and find his or her way out.

Although archaeologists have found most of the palace features and details mentioned by the ancient Greeks and others who visited it, they have not found any evidence of the labyrinth or the Minotaur. Why? Find or create an explanation.

Name_____

Pretest

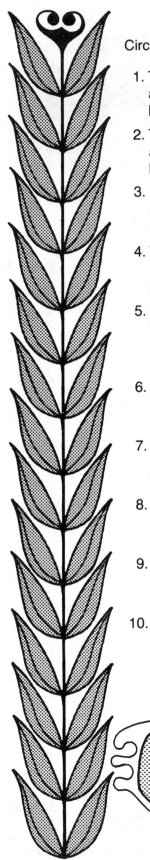

Circle the letter beside the best answer or the most appropriate response.

1. The oldest known European civilization was found
   a. in Mesoamerica.
   b. in Greece.
   c. in Egypt.
   d. on Crete.

2. This place can best be described as
   a. an island.
   b. a continent.
   c. a peninsula.
   d. a city.

3. It is located in the
   a. Pacific Ocean.
   b. Aegean Sea.
   c. Mediterranean Sea.
   d. Atlantic Ocean.

4. This civilization was originally thought to be
   a. gigantic.
   b. belligerent.
   c. philosophical.
   d. mythological.

5. The person whose work proved this ancient civilization to be fact, not fiction, was
   a. Thucydides.
   b. Sir Arthur Evans.
   c. Plato.
   d. John Lloyd Stephens.

6. He called this civilization
   a. Cretan.
   b. Mayan.
   c. Minoan.
   d. barbaric.

7. The creators of this civilization were masters of
   a. the seas.
   b. the skies.
   c. their fate.
   d. archaeology.

8. They were centuries ahead of their time when they invented
   a. the potter's wheel.
   b. the *shaduf.*
   c. indoor plumbing.
   d. hieroglyphics.

9. Their most important palace was built at
   a. Knossos.
   b. Bonampak.
   c. Giza.
   d. Rosetta.

10. Apparently, their remarkable civilization was destroyed by
    a. an atomic explosion.
    b. a revolution.
    c. a forest fire.
    d. a volcanic eruption.

Name_____

The Minoans of Crete

Off the coast of Greece in the Mediterranean Sea, halfway between the continents of Europe and Africa, lies the island of Crete. For at least three thousand years, people in that part of the world told fantastic stories about this island. According to these stories, it had once been the site of an impressive civilization. This civilization had been built by a remarkably intelligent and artistic group of people known as Minoans, after their most famous monarch, King Minos.

About King Minos the Greek historian Thucydides wrote, "He controlled the greater part of what is now called the Hellenic Sea; he ruled over the Cyclades [Aegean islands], in most of which he founded the first colonies, [and was] the first person to organize a navy." Despite Thucydides' writings, many scholars dismissed Minos and his people as mere myth.

Discoveries made early in this century and subsequent archaeological excavations have proved many of these fantastic stories to be true. Evidence now shows that, on Crete, the Minoans did establish one of Europe's first great civilizations. They farmed the fertile plains of their island and dominated the sea around it. In a huge fleet of ships, they traded throughout the Mediterranean area, exchanging grain, olive oil, and timber for the luxuries of Egypt and other neighboring lands. They built magnificent cities and splendid palaces.

Perhaps the most remarkable of these palaces was the one at Knossos. As a protection against the earthquakes which frequently rocked that region, the builders of this palace terraced it into the landscape. As a result, it was a maze of hallways, corridors, and staircases that linked storerooms and residential suites. These suites were elaborately decorated with frescoes. They were lighted and cooled by means of **light wells,** open shafts designed to admit light and air to the interior rooms of the building. At least one of these suites included a bathroom which was equipped with a toilet that flushed.

Obviously, the Minoans were an intelligent, inventive, and artistic people. Between 2500 and 1500 B.C., their influence spread throughout the smaller Aegean islands, known as the Cyclades; and Crete became a center of ideas for the ancient world.

Around 1470 B.C., much of the Minoan civilization was destroyed when a volcanic eruption on the island of Thera (which is also known as Santoríni) wracked the Aegean, submerging many harbors and changing forever the Minoan way of life. The palace at Knossos stood for a time and was occupied by Greek invaders; but by 1380 B.C., this palace lay in ruins, and mighty King Minos was but a memory.

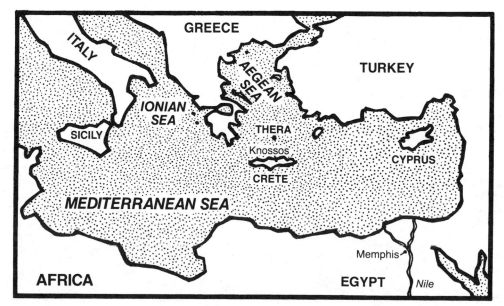

Name_____

Volcanic Activities

KN   1. **Volcanic Vocabulary:** Scientists who study volcanoes use a special vocabulary to describe what these mountains are and what they do. Before you begin your study of volcanoes, learn the meanings of these terms as they apply to volcanoes: **active, ash, cone, crater, dormant, eruption, extinct, lahar, lava, magma, pahoehoe, tsunami,** and **vent.** As you read about volcanoes, add other unfamiliar terms you encounter to this list.

KN CO   2. Around 1470 B.C., a volcanic eruption on the Aegean island of Thera devastated Crete. Do some research to learn more about volcanoes. What is a volcano? What parts does every volcano have? What causes a volcano to erupt? What happens when a volcano erupts? Share what you learn by means of a labeled diagram.

KN   3. Do some research to learn more about other volcanic eruptions and the civilizations they have threatened or destroyed. For example, you might read about the eruption of Mount Vesuvius in A.D. 79 or that of Krakatoa in A.D. 1883.

KN CO   4. There are about 850 active volcanoes in the world. More than three-fourths of these lie along a belt called the "Ring of Fire." Find out where this belt is located and trace it on a world map or globe.

KN   5. Some people think of a volcano as something that was formed hundreds or even thousands of years ago, and many volcanoes were. But one volcano was born as recently as February 20, 1943. On that date, Paricutín erupted from an otherwise unremarkable field in Mexico. Read about the birth of this relatively young volcano.

KN   6. Some people think that volcanic eruptions happened way back in history but don't happen now. Nothing could be further from the truth. To be sure, some volcanoes erupted long ago and have now become extinct, but others are active or are dormant and may once again become active. For example, both Mount St. Helens in Washington and Kilauea in Hawaii erupted in 1983; and Nevado del Ruiz erupted near Bogota, Colombia, on November 14, 1985. Use an almanac, encyclopedia, or other similar reference book to learn more about recent volcanic eruptions.

AP AN SY   7. Select ten volcanoes that interest you and make a chart showing the dates of their most recent eruptions. If possible, rate them according to the violence of their explosions. Share this information by means of a list, graph, or chart.

Finder of the Lost

Nearly everything that is now known about the ancient Minoan civilization can be traced to a spectacular discovery that was made less than one hundred years ago by Sir Arthur Evans. Evans, a British archaeologist, had been touring the Mediterranean area in search of ancient coins and seals. In Athens, Greece, he found some small, engraved stones from Crete which were covered with hieroglyphic writing in an unknown language. To Evans's practiced eye, the writing appeared to be extremely old, older than any that had previously been found in Europe. Could there have been a European civilization that predated the ones of which Evans and other scholars were aware? Evans thought so, and he vowed to find it.

In 1893, Arthur Evans began excavating at Knossos on the island of Crete. Almost immediately, his efforts were rewarded. He uncovered clay tablets with the same hieroglyphic writing that he had seen earlier on the stones in Athens. Evans also found huge walls and staircases that were parts of a seemingly endless palace. After excavating the palace, Evans carefully rebuilt it. Over the years, he reconstructed the lives of its occupants from the artifacts he unearthed and cataloged. He was convinced that the palace had been occupied continuously for thousands of years by the creators of a very advanced civilization.

When Evans could find no record of what the creators of this civilization had called it, he named it "Minoan" in honor of its mythological king, Minos. Evans spent more than forty years studying the lost Minoans he had found.

Name _____

Finder of the Lost
(continued)

Activities

KN
CO
1. Homer, a poet of ancient Greece, wrote two epic poems, the *Illiad* and the *Odyssey,* about the Trojan War. First, scan English translations of these poems for references to Crete. Then, summarize Homer's impressions of this ancient island and its people.

AN
SY
EV
2. For thousands of years, scientists and writers have speculated about a place called **Atlantis.** For example, Plato, a Greek philosopher, described Atlantis as an island continent in the western sea. According to Plato, this island continent had been home to a highly advanced civilization until its destruction by an earthquake. The creators of this civilization lived an idyllic existence on their fertile island. They built beautiful palaces and temples, devised systems for making hot and cold running water available and for removing sewage, and made ornaments of gold, silver, and bronze. Some scholars think that Plato's Atlantis might be Crete and that the civilization he described might be that of the Minoans. First, find out more about Atlantis. Then, evaluate this theory. From what you know or can learn, might Atlantis and Crete be two different names for the same place?

Beginnings

The beginnings of life on Crete are still something of a mystery. If Greek myths are to be believed, Crete's history reaches back to the birth of Zeus in a cave on that island. Relying on artifacts rather than on myths, archaeologists say that civilization began on Crete around 6000 B.C., when primitive farmers settled on the island's northern shore. These first settlers built mud-brick huts and grazed their cattle, sheep, and goats where the splendid Palace of Minos would later be constructed.

No one is certain where these early settlers came from. For a time, many people mistakenly thought that they were early Greeks. Actually, the Minoan civilization was older than the Greek one, and differences in the Greek and Minoan languages and customs prove that one of these civilizations is not simply an offshoot of the other.

For example, the early Greeks wore and admired beards, but not one Minoan artifact shows a Minoan with a beard. The Minoans were, in fact, clean shaven. A more plausible explanation seems to be that these first Cretans came from western Asia.

About 3000 B.C., more settlers came from this same region. These immigrants were descendants of a civilization that had evolved in the Middle East and had gradually spread westward across Asia and parts of Europe. They brought with them a new skill and a new age—the Bronze Age. They knew how to pound and shape metal—bronze, copper, silver, and gold—into tools, ornaments, and weapons. Crete provided the perfect setting for these small, graceful, dark-haired, dark-eyed artisans to become preeminent in their ancient world.

Activities

AP AN SY EV 1. Pretend that you are a scout sent to Crete from western Asia in 6000 B.C. to investigate the possibility of settling on that island. Before your trip, make a checklist of the needs of your people and the climatic conditions and natural resources you will look for. After your trip, write a report in which you describe the actual conditions you found and recommend whether the colony should settle in Crete or search elsewhere for more favorable conditions.

AP AN SY 2. Pretend that you are going to an island to found a colony. Use a series of charts, lists, and maps to explain your provisions and plans. Which island will you choose? How will you survive in this unfamiliar place? How many people will you take with you? What special skills will you and the other colonists need? What tools and equipment will you take? How will you travel? What rules and laws will be necessary to govern the colony? How will they be enforced?

Rulers of the Seas

The early settlers of Crete had come to that island by boat. They were experienced sailors with a fondness for the products of their homeland. Because of their personal skills and their island's climate, they had more grain, olives, olive oil, timber, wine, jewelry, vases, and bronze implements than they needed; and so they began to trade their surplus for the luxuries of other lands.

As the Minoan trading empire increased in size, more ships were needed to transport cargoes. To meet this need, the Minoans built an impressive fleet of sailing vessels, which regu-larly plied the waters to Egypt, the Aegean islands, and the countries along the eastern shores of the Mediterranean in search of imports as diverse as horses and lapis lazuli.

Because cargo ships were constantly being attacked by pirates, Crete's kings placed professional soldiers aboard each Cretan ship to guard its cargo and its crew. So successful was this practice that piracy virtually ceased. By rendering the Mediterranean safe for trade, the Minoans of Crete became for centuries the undisputed rulers of the seas.

Activities

KN
CO
EP
1. First, familiarize yourself with the meanings of these terms: **democracy, monarchy, oligarchy, theocracy,** and **thalassocracy.** Then, choose the one that best describes Crete and explain the reasons for your choice.

AN
SY
2. Both Egypt and Crete developed large shipping fleets so that they could engage in extensive foreign trade. Draw pictures or build models of Egyptian and Minoan oceangoing vessels. Compare them and list the similarities and differences between them.

Name_____

Bull-Leaping

In the palace at Knossos, there is an ancient wall painting that shows a huge spotted bull running straight toward a young woman who has grasped the animal's horns and stands poised for a leap onto its broad back. A boy teammate, who has already somersaulted gracefully onto the bull's back, is preparing to somersault again into the outstretched arms of another acrobat. These athletes are taking part in a Minoan sport now called **bull-leaping**.

Though facts are scarce, scholars have pieced together a description of bull-leaping. Working in teams, exceptionally brave and athletic youths—both boys and girls—captured bulls and brought them to palace courtyards. There, before enthusiastic crowds, the leapers would tease the bulls until they charged. As a bull came toward a leaper, he would grasp the animal's horns and lift himself onto the powerful creature's back. Once safely on the bull's broad back, the leaper would delight the crowd with incredible acrobatic feats.

Activities

AP 1. Draw a poster advertising an upcoming bull-leaping event.

AP 2. You are the announcer for the Annual All-Minoan Super Bull-Leap. Write a play-by-play account of this important sports event.

AP 3. Create a serious or humorous book of advice for bull-leaping trainees.

SY 4. Compare Minoan bull-leaping with Spanish bullfighting. In what ways are these two sports similar? In what ways are they different?

Name_____

King Minos and the Minotaur

Fabulous tales were told of the island of Crete and of its legendary king, Minos. King Minos was a son of the greatest of all Greek gods, Zeus. With a fleet of sturdy sailing vessels, Minos controlled the seas and colonized the neighboring islands. By means of trade and tribute, he amassed great wealth.

King Minos had a wife named Pasiphae. To show his love for his queen, Minos used some of his wealth to build a palace for her at Knossos. In planning this magnificent structure, no detail was overlooked; in constructing it, no expense was spared. When, at last, the palace was finished, it dazzled the known world with its painted walls, winding staircases, and running water.

As you might expect, life in so beautiful a setting passed agreeably for many years; but unfortunately, Minos and his queen did not live happily ever after. Because Crete was an island in the midst of a tumultuous ocean, Minos always took great pains to honor Poseidon, the god of the sea, with regular sacrifices. On one such occasion, however, Poseidon demanded a bull that Minos prized very highly. When the king brashly refused the god's request, Poseidon grew very angry. In his rage, the deity caused the ocean depths to shake and the waves to swell and crash relentlessly upon the shores of the fragile island.

After a time, Poseidon's rage gave way to a desire for revenge. When Pasiphae grew great with child and Minos prayed for a son, Poseidon caused the queen to bear a hideous monster. Half man and half bull, this monster was called the Minotaur to indicate that it was Minos's bull. In shame and fear, Minos had his cunning craftsman, Daedalus, build an intricate maze of walled pathways, called a **labyrinth,** below his palace to house the savage beast.

King Minos and the Minotaur
(continued)

Now the Minotaur was not particularly pleased with this arrangement and would frequently paw the ground with his enormous hooves, butt the walls with his massive head, and snort loudly through his flaring nostrils. When he did so, the entire palace would shake, causing its occupants to tremble in fear.

Minos searched in vain for ways to pacify the ferocious beast. The king ordered his servants to feed the Minotaur bales of the sweetest hay. He had his court musicians play strains of the most soothing music, but all to no avail. Rather than being placated by the king's efforts, the Minotaur was irritated by them and grew more and more enraged.

Now Minos and Pasiphae had a son named Androgeos, whom they loved as dearly as any parents could love a son. From his boyhood, Androgeos had been a gifted athlete and had given his doting parents much reason to be proud. When Androgeos competed in the Panathenic Games at Athens, Greece, he ably defeated all of his opponents. Aegeus, the king of Athens, feared the youth's strength and was jealous of his success. In consequence, he ordered some of his soldiers to kill the Cretan youth.

When Minos learned of his son's death, he was grief stricken. Pasiphae tried to comfort her husband, but he was inconsolable. To avenge the cold-blooded murder of his beloved son, the bereaved king made war on the Athenians. Minos was victorious. As a condition of Athenian surrender, he compelled Aegeus to send to Crete every year seven youths and seven maidens, as a tribute.

When an Athenian ship bearing the first annual tribute sailed into the Cretan harbor, King Minos had the hapless youths imprisoned in the labyrinth with the Minotaur. There they wandered aimlessly until, one by one, the bloodthirsty beast discovered and devoured them and, at last, was quiet for a time.

With the Minotaur thus appeased, King Minos and Queen Pasiphae lived in relative calm, basking in the luxury of their magnificent palace and the lushness of their island paradise.

Ariadne and Theseus

King Minos and Pasiphae also had a daughter named Ariadne. The climate of Crete must have agreed with the girl; for each day as she played in the island sun, she grew more and more beautiful. Minos and Pasiphae watched her with pride and spoke often of her future as the wife of a wealthy Aegean prince.

Aegeus, the king of Athens, had a son named Theseus, who was as brave as he was handsome. To prove himself worthy of his father's throne, the young prince killed the Marathonian bull, which had been terrorizing the Athenian countryside, and then volunteered to go as one of the seven youths to Crete.

Now it had become the custom for the seven Athenian youths and the seven Athenian maidens who were sent as an annual tribute to be paraded through the streets of Crete as part of a glorious victory celebration before they were sealed forever in the labyrinth. On this particular occasion, one of the Cretans watching the festivities was Ariadne. As the group of fourteen approached the palace, her sparkling dark eyes fell on Theseus. After he had passed, the Cretan princess realized that she was in love with the Athenian prince.

Quickly the smitten girl ran to her father's suite where she asked that one Athenian youth be spared; but the king, recalling all too vividly the brutal murder of his beloved son, refused her request. Determined to do something, the desperate princess sought out Daedalus, the craftsman who had designed the labyrinth, and asked him to help her. Fearing the king's wrath,

Daedalus at first refused; but the girl continued to plead until the softhearted man could hold out no longer. He agreed to give Ariadne a sword for Theseus so that the prince would not have to face the Minotaur unarmed.

But Ariadne was not satisfied. She explained to Daedalus that she wanted not only to save the handsome prince's life but to marry him as well. Then she asked Daedalus to reveal the secrets of his labyrinth to her. Concerned that his complicity might be discovered if he complied with the girl's request, Daedalus hastily pressed a spool of thread into her hand, telling her to give it to Theseus and instruct him to unwind it as he walked into the labyrinth so that he could follow it to find his way back along the puzzling pathways of the maze.

Ariadne did as she had been told, and Theseus was successful. He returned from the labyrinth, lifted the waiting Ariadne in his arms, and carried her to an Athenian ship that was standing at anchor in the harbor nearby. Together, they sailed back to Athens. In his great relief and unbounded joy, Theseus forgot that his father had instructed him to hoist a white sail as he approached the Athenian shore to signal his success. When Aegeus did not see the agreed-upon sign, he presumed that his son had fallen victim to the Minotaur like all of the other Athenian youths before him. Overcome with grief, the heartbroken king hurled himself into the sea, where he drowned. Thus, Theseus and his Cretan bride came to rule Athens.

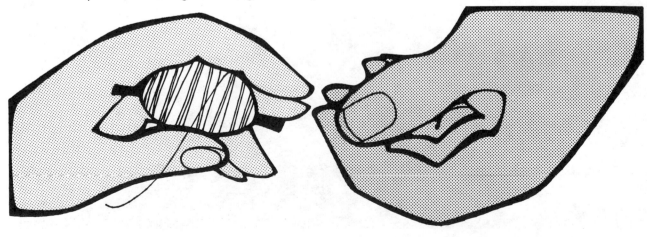

Name _____

Mythological Activity Sheet

co
AP
AN
1. Ancient people who were awed by natural phenomena developed myths to explain what they could not understand. For example, when the earth beneath Knossos rumbled and the palace shook, mythmakers blamed an angry and imprisoned beast, the Minotaur. What natural phenomena might have caused these events? Explain your answer.

KN
CO
2. The Greek word **pantheios** means "of all gods." From this Greek word comes the English word **pantheon,** the name given to the officially recognized gods of a people. Do some research to learn more about Zeus, Hera, and the other gods and goddesses who were members of the ancient Greek pantheon.

co
AP
AN
3. Although the Greek and Minoan civilizations were separate, Greek myths contain many references to Crete, to kings who ruled that island, and to events that happened there. It is generally believed that these Greek myths date from 1500 B.C. How would you account for the strong influence of Crete on Greek mythology?

AP
4. Zeus, Hera, and other Greek deities purportedly lived atop Mount Olympus, the highest peak in Greece. Pretend that you are the author of a "personals" column for a newspaper called the *Mount Olympus Monitor.* Choose deities and heroes from Greek mythology, compose a letter each one might write, and provide an appropriate response. For example, the wood nymph Echo might write of her love for Narcissus and ask how she should go about telling the handsome youth of her feelings and persuading him to take a romantic interest in her.

AP
AN
5. While myths are not totally true, they may be based on fact or contain some element of truth. For example, when Sir Arthur Evans began looking for the Palace of King Minos, he made his excavations at Knossos, where myths said that the palace had once stood. As a result of Evans's extensive studies, many of the ancient and fabulous stories about Minos and Crete have been confirmed. In view of this fact, discuss the relationship between fact and fiction in myth.

"Cunning Craftsman"

In the days of King Minos, as in other times before and since, it was the custom for men of wealth and influence to hire men of talent and ingenuity to beautify their surroundings and to make their lives more enjoyable. Crete's rich and powerful king was no exception to this custom.

Among the people King Minos hired was Daedalus, an Athenian sculptor and inventor who had fled his native Greece after being accused of murder. Daedalus, whose name means "cunning craftsman," rewarded his Cretan patron by designing the dazzling palace at Knossos. Its many stories set atop impressive regiments of columns, its winding staircases, and its running water were all expressions of Daedalus's creative genius. And when King Minos's wife Pasiphae gave birth to the Minotaur, Daedalus designed and supervised construction of the intricate maze of passageways known as the labyrinth, in which this fearsome beast could be safely housed.

According to myth, Daedalus also created a gigantic bronze robot named Talos. This robot's primary purpose was to protect Crete from its enemies, a task for which Talos was well suited. Unlike his human counterparts, the robot did not tire. Three times each day, he made a trip around the island, surveying the coastline for any suspicious activity. While Talos was on these rounds, flames leaped from his gaping mouth, and boulders large enough to sink a ship were effortlessly tossed by his enormous arms. At times, the robot would stand in fire until his shiny metal surface glowed red-hot. Then, he would grasp unwelcome guests in a searing and deadly embrace. As you might imagine, stories about Talos spread quickly to neighboring nations and discouraged all but the bravest would-be invaders.

Although Daedalus served Minos long and well, he and the king frequently disagreed. During one of their more heated quarrels, Minos became so angry that he had Daedalus and his son, Icarus, imprisoned in a palace tower. To escape, the clever Daedalus collected the large feathers dropped by seabirds and, using beeswax as an adhesive, fashioned them into wings. When, at last, the wings were finished, Daedalus and Icarus put them on. As they did so, the wary father cautioned his son to stay close and to avoid danger. Icarus readily agreed; but once in the sky, he forgot his father's warnings. Instead of following Daedalus carefully to safety, Icarus darted about, reveling in his new-found freedom. Eventually, when the heedless boy flew too high, the sun softened the beeswax, causing the feathers to fall from his wings. As his father watched in horror, the helpless boy plummeted into the sea and was drowned. Heartbroken, Daedalus flew on alone and never again returned to Crete.

Name＿＿＿＿＿＿＿＿＿＿＿＿＿＿＿＿＿

"Cunning Craftsman" Activity Sheet

AP
AN

1. The name Daedalus means "cunning craftsman." Familiarize yourself with the meanings of the words **cunning** and **craftsman,** and then decide whether or not you think that they comprise an appropriate name for this Athenian sculptor and inventor. Explain the reasons for your decision.

AP

2. First, look at pictures of ancient ballistic machines and of modern robotic devices. Then, decide what Talos might have looked like. Finally, draw and label a diagram or a picture of this remarkable defensive weapon.

SY
EV

3. The word **robot** was first used more than sixty years ago by Karel Čapek, a Czechoslovakian writer, in his play *R.U.R.,* or *Rossum's Universal Robots.* Čapek used the Czechoslovakian word *roboto*, which means "compulsory labor" or "slave," to describe the unusual mechanical creatures in his play. In Čapek's drama, problems arise when the mechanistic robots are given human feelings. Should Daedalus have given feelings to Talos? On a separate sheet of paper, write a paragraph in which you answer this question and give reasons for your answer.

AN
SY
EV

4. The myths about Daedalus make him seem too clever to be true, too ingenious ever to have really existed—unless you are familiar with the work of Leonardo da Vinci. Leonardo, who was born in 1452 and died in 1519, spent his lifetime observing, questioning, discovering, experimenting, and inventing. He designed the first airplane, was the first to develop the concept of the helicopter, and was the first to invent the diving suit. Working from Leonardo's labeled diagrams and detailed notes and sketches, Italian engineers have constructed two hundred working models of his various inventions. First, do some research to learn more about Leonardo da Vinci. Then, compare Leonardo with Daedalus. Finally, decide whether you think that Daedalus was historical or merely mythological and discuss the reasons for your decision.

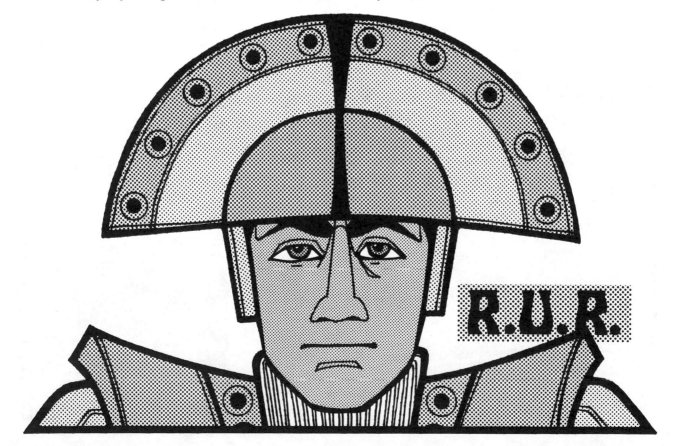

The Palace at Knossos

Nearly four thousand years ago, the Minoans began building magnificent palaces for their rulers. These buildings were less remarkable for their architectural beauty than for their size and the amazing innovations they contained. The grandest of all of these palaces was the home of King Minos at Knossos.

Built in wings around a huge open courtyard, the palace at Knossos covered more than six square acres and was about the same size as England's Buckingham Palace. On the west were all of the governmental offices and religious shrines. On the north were extensive workshops for use by the king's artists and craftsmen. And on the east were the royal apartments. Although these apartments are three or four stories tall, they appear to be only one story high because two of the stories are underground. By removing part of a hill and building below ground level, the ingenious Minoans were able to take advantage of both the view and the breeze.

The palace at Knossos contained many large, light-filled rooms connected by wide corridors. It was equipped with an incredibly modern plumbing system by which running water was carried to tubs, sinks, and flush toilets in splendid bathrooms. In addition, excavators found many hidden staircases and secret passageways. So far, however, they have not found any evidence of the labyrinth or of its terrifying occupant, the Minotaur. For this reason, no one knows where the Greeks got the idea that this intricate chamber existed. Perhaps Greek visitors found the arrangement of rooms within the palace confusing and thought it had been intentionally designed to be so. Scholars have suggested that the misunderstanding may have been the result of a difference in word meaning. Because the double ax was an important religious symbol to the Minoans, they referred to their palace as "a house of the double ax," or **labyrinthos.** To the Greeks, this same word meant "a large building with intricate and confusing passageways" or, in other words, "a maze."

The Palace at Knossos Activity Sheet

CO 1. First, find out where the royal occupants of the palace at Knossos hid their treasure. Then, invent a
AP   security system for this storage area. Explain your system by means of labeled drawings and/or
       diagrams.

CO 2. Do some additional research to learn more about the palace at Knossos. Then, imagine that you
AP   are an ancient visitor to this palace. Write a letter to a friend in which you describe this amazing
       structure in some detail.

CO 3. Write an illustrated feature article for *Palace and Garden* or *Palace Beautiful* magazine in which
AP   you picture and describe a Minoan palace.

CO 4. Pretend that you are a very wealthy monarch on an island. Think about the building in which you
AP   would like to live. First, list the features you would want this building to include. Then, draw pictures
       and floor plans of this structure.

AN 5. By means of pictures and diagrams, compare a Minoan palace with a similar structure built by the
SY   Egyptians or the Greeks. In what ways are they similar? In what ways are they different? Can the
       differences you have observed by explained primarily in terms of function or of the differences in
       ideas about beauty subscribed to by these cultures? Explain your answer.

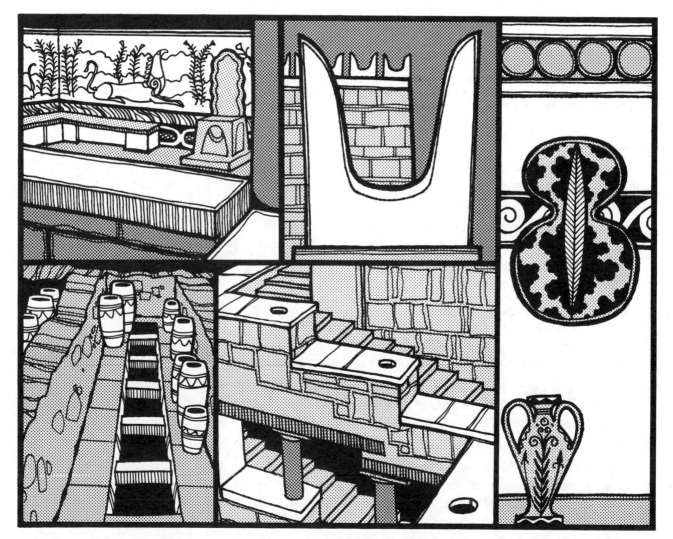

Name_____

The Sacred Caves

One curious aspect of Minoan culture is the absence of temples. The creators of many other ancient civilizations—for example, the Egyptians and the Maya—spent years building elaborate structures in which their deities could live and be worshiped. Why are there no such structures on Crete?

Crete is an island made mostly of limestone, a sedimentary rock in which water hollows out grottoes and carves intricate passageways. The Minoans thought of these caves as sacred and used them as places in which to perform religious ceremonies and leave offerings. These ancient inhabitants of Crete had no reason to erect temples because nature had already done that job for them.

Archaeologists have excavated several Cretan caves. The richest of these is the Arkalochori Cave, some twelve miles south of Knossos. It was apparently used as a sanctuary from 2000 B.C. until 1450 B.C., when an earthquake caused its roof to fall in. Within this cave, villagers and scholars have found bronze weapons, pottery, and sacred double axes.

Another Cretan cave that was apparently used for worship is the Psychro Cave, discovered by peasants in 1883. Located about ten miles east of Arkalochori, this enormous cave is supposed to be the one in which Zeus was born and the one in which King Minos found the sacred Laws. Psychro Cave was originally composed of an upper and a lower grotto. In the upper grotto, archaeologists found animal bones, bronzes, and pottery. The lower grotto yielded dagger blades, double axes, fibulae, and statuettes all made of bronze.

For thousands of years, Minoan artifacts lay hidden deep within these sacred caves. Excavations at cave sites have yielded a wealth of knowledge about Minoan life and customs.

Activities

KN 1. Limestone caverns like the ones on Crete are found in several places in the United States. Do some research to learn more about Carlsbad Caverns in New Mexico, Luray Caverns in Virginia, or Mammoth Cave in Kentucky.

KN 2. **Stalagmites** and **stalactites** are often found in limestone caverns. What are they and how are they formed?

KN
CO 3. Would you like to be a **spelunker**? Explain what one is, what one does, and why you would or would not like to do it.

KN
CO 4. The caves on Crete were formed by the action of organic acids on deposits of limestone. Limestone is a sedimentary rock composed wholly or in large part of a chemical compound called calcium carbonate. Read to find out more about this compound and exactly how it is changed by organic acids. Then explain or demonstrate this process.

KN
CO 5. Among the bronze artifacts found in Psychro Cave was something called a **fibula.** Do some research to discover what an ancient fibula looked like and how this word is used today. Share what you learn by means of labeled diagrams and sketches.

AP 6. Using information contained in "The Birth of Zeus" on page 93, write a myth to explain an earthquake, famine, flood, or volcanic eruption.

AP 7. Look up the meanings of the following twelve words: **deities, divert, emetic, Hellenic, mar, noxious, nuptial, prediction, prophecy, regurgitate, titan, tyrannical.** Use them in sentences or in a story.

The Birth of Zeus

The Minoans and Greeks shared many myths. According to one of these myths, the god Zeus was born in a cave on the island of Crete. Here is an account of that remarkable birth.

All of the known gods and goddesses originated with Father Heaven and Mother Earth, who were also known as Uranus and Gaea. Uranus and Gaea bore twelve children, six sons and six daughters. Together, these superbeings were called the Titans; and among them were the Cyclopes, the Hecatoncheires, a son Cronos, and a daughter Rhea.

Uranus was a demanding husband and a tyrannical father who imprisoned his children beneath the earth in a place more remote and terrible than Hell. When, at last, Gaea could bear her husband's cruelty no longer, she helped Cronos overthrow his father and become ruler of the universe.

Cronos then married his sister, Rhea; but their nuptial happiness was marred by Gaea's prediction that one of Cronos's children would overthrow him exactly as he had overthrown Uranus. To protect himself from this fearsome prophecy, Cronos swallowed each of his first five children—Hestia, Demeter, Hera, Hades, and Poseidon—immediately after birth.

Although Rhea loved her husband, she could not bear to see him destroy another of her children. When she became pregnant for the sixth time, she decided to protect her unborn child from the terrible fate that had befallen the others. While Cronos's gaze was diverted, Rhea slipped away to a remote island cave, where she gave birth to a baby boy, whom she named Zeus. Keeping the infant carefully hidden on earth, Rhea returned to Cronos's side, told him of the birth, and tricked him into swallowing a rock instead of the child.

As the years went by Zeus grew to be a strong and handsome young man. When he was old enough, Rhea brought him to the palace to be a cupbearer for his unsuspecting father. In this capacity, the youth's primary task was to fill, carry, and protect the cup from which his father drank. One night, Rhea mixed a powerful emetic for Cronos, put it in his cup, and persuaded Zeus to serve it to his father. Cronos, thinking that the noxious mixture was wine, drank it and promptly regurgitated his five other children, now fully grown.

Zeus and his two brothers waged a mighty war against Cronos and the other Titans for control of the universe. When Zeus and his allies were finally victorious, they imprisoned Cronos and the other Titans within the earth, where their continuing struggle to free themselves still causes gentle rumblings and, from time to time, violent quakes.

Zeus and his brothers then divided the government of the universe among them. To Hades was given the lower world so that he became ruler over all of the minerals and treasures within the earth and giver of all wealth. To Poseidon was given the earth, both its land and its seas. To Zeus was given the heavens. As for the three sisters, Hestia, the first-born of Rhea, became the goddess of home and of the fire burning on the hearth. Demeter became goddess of the fruits of the earth, especially corn, and of the harvest. Hera became goddess of womanhood and marriage and, as the wife of Zeus, queen of the gods. Together, these six deities went to live on Mount Olympus, the highest peak in Greece, from where they ruled the entire Hellenic universe.

Name_____

Fun-Filled Frescoes

The Minoans began decorating the walls and ceilings of their important buildings as long ago as 2000 B.C. Painting directly on the wet plaster in red-orange, green, blue, gold, cream, and other colors, they created **frescoes** that depict lifelike people, powerful land animals, playful sea creatures, and graceful flowers. Among their favorite subjects were bulls, dolphins, and octopuses. The resulting scenes reflected the joy and contentment that characterized Minoan life. These scenes, full of energy and movement, were usually contained within borders of stylized or geometric designs. Because Minoan artists were very adept at capturing the essential nature of their subjects, infusing them with life, and portraying them in exuberant colors, their work was in great demand throughout the ancient world.

Activities

AP 1. First, study color prints of Minoan paintings. Then, use the Minoan palette to paint a picture of a subject that pleases you.

CO
AN 2. Compare the Maya and Minoan palettes. In what ways are they similar? In what ways are they different? Explain the ways in which environment might determine or influence color choice.
SY

AN 3. Compare pictures of Maya and Minoan murals. In what ways are the colors, lines, subjects, and styles of these wall paintings similar? In what ways are they different? What differences in life-style and attitude might have caused these differences in artistic expression?
SY

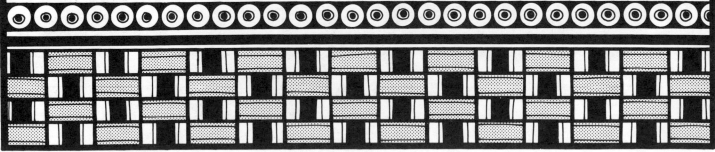

Name _____

Pottery Activity Sheet

KN
CO 1. Familiarize yourself with the meanings of these twenty-two terms, which all have something to do
with pottery making:

bone china	greenware
bone-dry	kiln
ceramics	porcelain
ceramist	porcelaneous
clay	potter
coil method	potter's wheel
cone	raku ware
dry	slab method
earthenware	slip
fire	stoneware
glaze	terra-cotta

KN
CO 2. First, read about the process by which clay is transformed into pottery. Then, create a chart on
which you describe and illustrate the separate steps in this process.

KN
CO 3. Clay is an earthy material that is soft and malleable when moist but rock hard and rigid when dry. It
is composed of aluminum silicates and other minerals. Read to learn more about the chemical
composition of clays and glazes.

AP 4. Obtain some modeling or potter's clay. Using either the coil or slab method, form it into plates,
bowls, vases, or figurines.

KN
CO 5. Make a chart showing how various combinations of minerals are used to give different kinds of
ceramic ware their characteristic appearance, color, hardness, and texture.

AP 6. Use color and line to decorate the Minoan pitcher pictured on page 96.

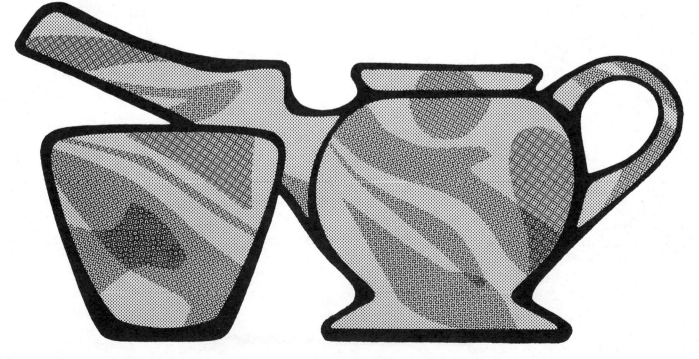

Name _____

Minoan Pitcher

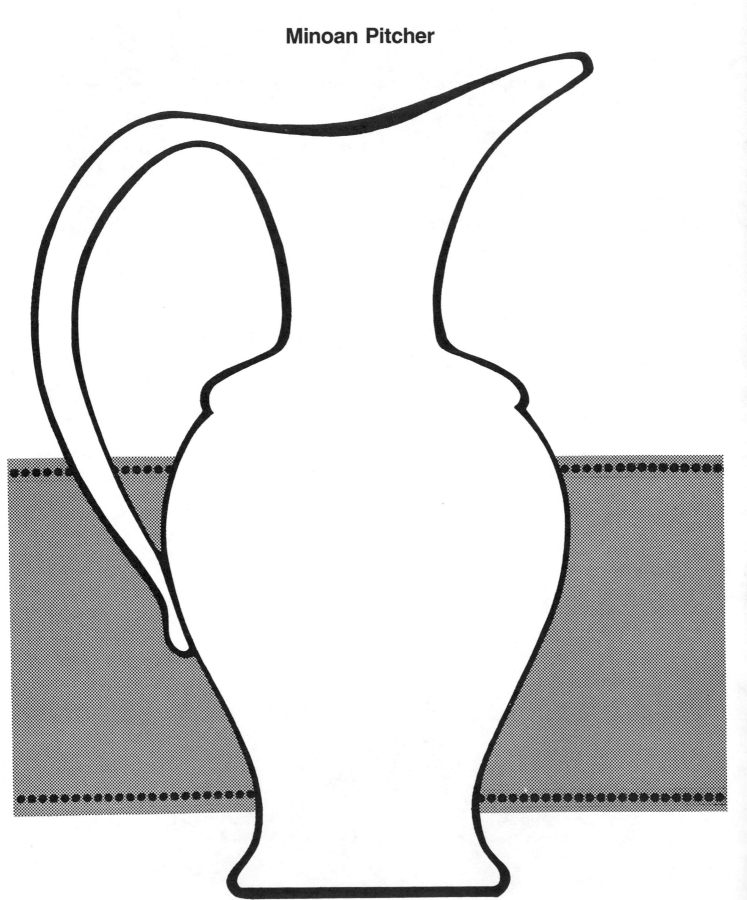

Name_____

Minoan Writing

Despite nearly one hundred years of excavation and study, much about the Minoans remains a mystery. For example, scholars know very little about their history or their thoughts and have looked to Minoan writing to fill in the vast information gaps left by artifacts and ruins.

The Minoans wrote by carving symbols into slabs of wet clay. Apparently, they never intended to preserve these tablets. Instead, each one was kept only as long as the information on it was needed. When information became obsolete, the tablets on which it had been written were pulped. Fortunately, many of these Minoan tablets were accidentally involved in a fire, which hardened and preserved them.

So far, at least three different scripts have been identified on clay tablets and seal stones found throughout Crete. The earliest of these is a **hieroglyphic script** that was in use from 2000 to 1600 B.C. and may have been introduced from Syria. In this script, as in early Egyptian hieroglyphics, pictorial symbols are used to represent common objects, such as a head, a hand, a fish, a star, and a double ax.

The second script is **Linear A**, which was used from 1900 B.C. until the fall of the palaces around 1450 B.C. In this simplification of the earlier hieroglyphic script, many of the carefully drawn hieroglyphs have become hastily jotted squiggles. Although scholars have been unable to decipher Linear A, they have concluded that its picture-symbols stand for syllables in a spoken language that is *not* Greek.

More important to our understanding of Minoan culture is a script called **Linear B**. This script was in use at Knossos between 1450 and 1400 B.C., during the last days of the palaces. Examples of it are not found anywhere else on Crete but have been discovered in the Mycenaean palaces of Greece. Linear B consists of eighty-seven symbols and a number of ideograms. Though it was derived independently from the earlier hieroglyphic script, it resembles Linear A in many ways. Interestingly enough, Linear B has been deciphered, and the language written in it has been identified as a primitive form of Greek.

Linear B is the only one of the three Minoan scripts that has been deciphered. Ordinarily, messages written in an unknown script cannot be deciphered unless a **bilingual**—that is, a document on which the message is written in both a known and the unknown language—is found. A bilingual enables scholars to equate the symbols of the unfamiliar language with symbols and words in the familiar one and, thus, to **translate** the message. The Rosetta stone is the bilingual that made possible the decipherment of Egyptian hieroglyphics.

The man who deciphered Linear B was not a language scholar and did not have a bilingual. What he did have was a brilliant intellect, an unquenchable thirst for knowledge about Knossos, and an undying interest in Minoan writing. That man was Michael Ventris, an English architect.

In 1936, as a boy, Ventris had visited an exhibition at which Sir Arthur Evans lectured about the nearly four thousand Linear B tablets he had unearthed at Knossos. Then and there, Ventris resolved to decipher Linear B and announced sixteen years later that he had, in fact, done so.

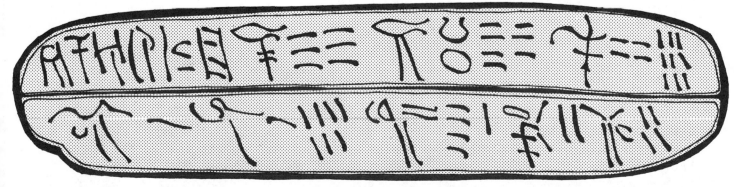

Minoan Writing
(continued)

Forced to work without a bilingual because none existed or had been found, Ventris relied instead on his acquaintance with wartime code-breaking techniques. Meticulously, he analyzed the frequency and relative position of each symbol. From his analysis, he concluded that there were too few symbols for Linear B to be picture writing and too many symbols for this script to be an alphabet. Instead, he decided, Linear B was a **syllabary**, a set of written symbols or characters that each stood for a different spoken syllable. Ventris then worked out a set of sound values for the Linear B symbols which made sense in Greek. His decipherment was published in the *Journal of Hellenic Studies* in 1953.

Although Michael Ventris's accomplishment is an important one, the tablets written in Linear B tell us little about either Minoan history or Minoan thought. The messages on them are not diary entries, essays, or letters. Instead, they are dedications to the gods and government records—lists of armaments, of palace stores, and of collected taxes.

Activities

KN
CO
1. A possible fourth Minoan script has been found on the Phaestos Disc. Do some research to discover what the Phaestos Disc is, where and when it was found, and what sort of writing appears on its surface.

CO
AP
AN
2. At the same time that the Minoans were scratching their messages into the surfaces of clay tablets, the Egyptians were writing with ink on papyrus. Might the Minoans have used papyrus? If so, why wasn't any found in the ruins on Crete? If not, what reasons might account for their failure to do so?

CO
AP
AN
3. Some scholars have suggested that the Minoans might have used clay tablets for their public records and papyrus for their private thoughts and personal correspondence. If they did so, what conditions on Crete might account for archaeologists' failure to find codices, scrolls, or other similar papyrus documents?

CO
AP
AN
EV
4. Much of what is important in our culture is recorded on paper—news and history, calculations and measurements, facts and fiction. Imagine that civilization as we know it has been destroyed by a major catastrophe of some sort. As the years pass, all of the paper that once reflected our culture is likewise destroyed by fire, moisture, insects, and animals. Archaeologists coming upon the scene several thousand years later find only those messages that were inscribed on metal or engraved in stone. What would they find? What might they conclude about our culture from these findings? How accurate or inaccurate might their conclusions be?

Name_____

Minoan Houses

How, after centuries of damage and destruction by the elements, can anyone tell anything about the dwellings of the ordinary citizens of a vanished civilization? Sometimes, archaeologists are forced to make educated guesses based on what they know about the climate and the available building materials; however, with the Minoans, scholars have been more fortunate. At Knossos, they found an ancient wooden storage chest fitted with clay panels on which were pictured the homes of ordinary people. By looking at these pictures, scholars have been able to piece together a composite idea of what many Minoan dwellings probably looked like.

Apparently, Minoan homes were tall, flat-roofed, boxlike buildings constructed of clay bricks, plaster, or stone. They were two to four stories high and consisted of six to twelve rooms arranged around an open courtyard. They featured indoor bathrooms with running water but no kitchens because most of the cooking was done outside, in the courtyard. Openings in the walls—doors and windows—were usually square or rectangular in shape. Frequently, the exterior walls were decorated with colorful patterns, especially horizontal stripes. The interior walls of these homes were also painted to reflect the cheerful, fun-loving personalities of their owners.

Minoan Houses Activity Sheet

KN
CO
AP

1. Pretend that you are a real estate agent on ancient Crete. Write and illustrate a pamphlet or brochure showing the different types of housing that are available to your clients. Include both ordinary houses and palaces.

KN
CO
AP

2. Plan and construct a model of a Minoan house or palace. For the walls, use clay, cardboard, styrofoam cubes, or empty shoe boxes. For the door and window frames, consider balsa wood, cardboard pieces, or Popsicle sticks. Paint with acrylic or tempera paint to obtain the color and texture you want. Consider stacking shoe boxes side on side to create houses that are several stories high. Within the boxes, make separate dioramas to show what activities might have taken place on each floor of a Minoan house.

AN
SY

3. Compare a Minoan palace with a palace or mansion in use today. In what ways are they similar? In what ways are they different?

AN
SY
EV

4. Compare a Minoan house with the structure in which you live. In what ways are they similar? In what ways are they different? After considering the similarities and differences, which one do you prefer? Why?

AN
SY
EV

5. Think about the characteristics of an average Minoan home. Using a scale of one to ten, rate this style of dwelling for construction and use in each of the following environments: (a) northern or Arctic regions with extremely low temperatures and heavy snowfall; (b) desert regions with very hot days, chilly nights, negligible rainfall, and possible blowing sand; (c) coastal areas with strong winds; (d) tropical rain forests, and (e) regions subject to violent earthquakes. Compare actual homes built in these areas with the average Minoan home. In what ways are they similar? In what ways are they different? Why?

Name _____

Elegant Fashions

On a breezy summer night in 1480 B.C., a wealthy young Minoan couple make their way along a rocky Cretan pathway toward a lavish party in the palace at Knossos. Knowing that hundreds of Minoan and foreign dignitaries have been invited, the two young Minoans have taken special care with their appearances. Both of them are keenly aware that the people of Crete are famous for their elegant fashions.

The man, who is clean shaven, wears a short, wraparound skirt and fancy leather sandals. A wide metal belt accentuates his narrow, seventeen-inch waist. On his bare neck, arms, and chest are a collar, arm bands, bracelets, and a breastplate crafted of gold, silver, and precious gems.

The woman's beautifully embroidered gown is the result of one entire month of work by a well-known seamstress. The gown has a low-cut neckline, a tight waist, a full, floor-length skirt, and long, puffy sleeves. On her feet the woman wears soft leather slippers. Her dark, curly hair has been carefully arranged by a clever servant in a very elaborate style; and her neck, arms, and hair glitter with sparkling jewels.

As the man and his wife move among the other party guests, they are convinced that few people are as well-dressed and stylish as they.

Name _____

Elegant Fashions Activity Sheet

CO
AP 1. Write and illustrate a fashion column for the *Minoan Monitor.*

CO
AP 2. Use the party mentioned on page 101 as the basis for writing a society column for the newspaper named above.

CO
AP
AN 3. Minoan women wore makeup. First, do some research to learn what substances and colors they used and how these were applied. Then, draw a picture of a Minoan woman before and after a makeup makeover.

AN
SY 4. Compare clothing worn by the Minoans with that worn by citizens of another ancient culture, for example, the Egyptians or the Maya. In what ways are they similar? In what ways are they different? Which ones of these differences are the result of differences in climate and/or available materials? Which ones of these differences reflect differences in prevailing attitudes?

Name_____

Any-Culture Paper Dolls

KN
CO
AP
Dress the paper dolls drawn below in ancient Egyptian, Maya, or Minoan costumes. In creating the appropriate look, consider not only clothing and shoes but also hairstyle, headdress, and jewelry. Don't forget makeup, body paint, and tattoos.

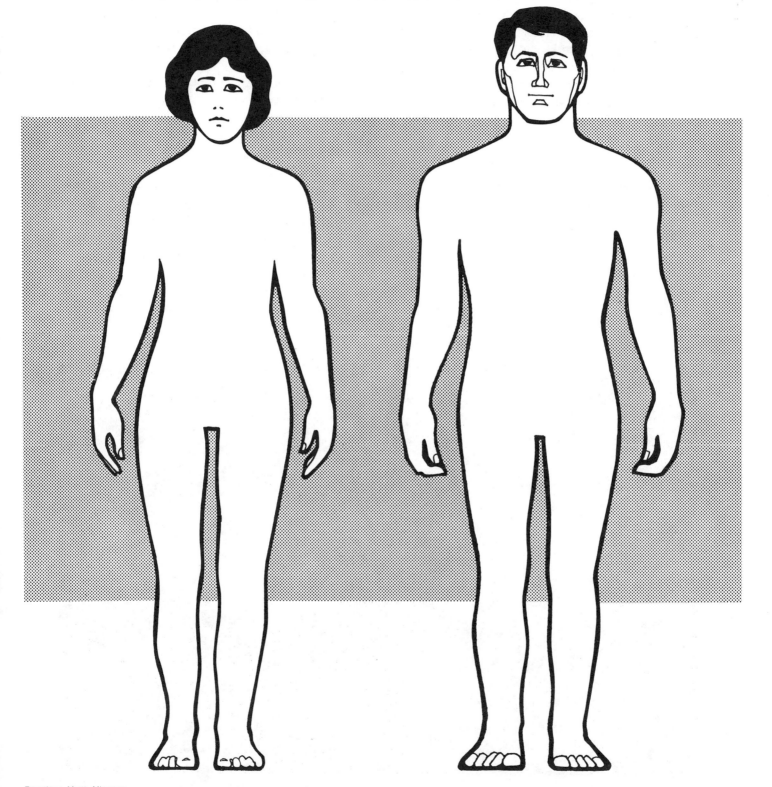

The Final Chapter

When archaeologists excavated the palace at Knossos, they found evidence that some great disaster had struck around 1400 B.C. Smoke stains on palace walls indicated that there had been a large fire. Overturned and scattered ritual vessels suggested that their panicked users had left hastily, perhaps to escape crumbling walls or rapidly advancing flames. The exact nature and cause of this disaster are unknown, and its relationship to the end of Minoan civilization is unexplained; but scholars have offered several theories.

After six centuries of advanced civilization—marked by freedom and prosperity, peace and stability—a major change took place. Crete was no longer purely Minoan; Knossos was occupied by Mycenaeans.

The Mycenaeans were a powerful, blond, equestrian people who introduced horses to the Mediterranean area. Scholars are uncertain about the extent to which the Mycenaeans influenced and controlled Minoan life, but evidence strongly suggests that the two cultures coexisted by means of an arrangement that gave the newcomers the upper hand. This theory is supported by the fact that, during this period, Minoan records were kept in the script called Linear B, which was being used at the same time by the Mycenaeans on the Greek mainland.

During the ensuing fifty-year period of coexistence, palace life remained as luxurious as it had been before; but it was tinged by subtle change. For the first time, horses and chariots appeared in palace inventories; and there was an increased concern with weapons and other military matters.

If archaeological evidence suggests a generation or two of peaceful coexistence, what spelled the end for the Minoans? Was it a devastating earthquake? Was it an attempted revolt by native Minoans against their Mycenaean overlords? Or was it a crushing invasion by a rival group of Greeks who tried to wrest control of Crete from the Mycenaeans? No one knows for certain.

The Final Chapter Activity Sheet

KN
CO
AP

1. Write a myth to explain the destruction of Minoan civilization on Crete. In your myth, include a proud ruler, an angry god, and a hero or heroine who helps others escape miraculously to the safety of another land.

KN
CO
AP
AN

2. At least three explanations have been offered for the destruction of Minoan palaces and, subsequently, of Minoan civilization: (1) that a natural disaster destroyed the buildings, and invading Mycenaeans infiltrated Minoan culture, weakening its fabric; (2) that the palaces were destroyed during an initial Greek invasion; and (3) that the palaces were destroyed as one group of Greeks fought against another group of Greeks, who had already subdued the Minoans and occupied their important cities. Select one of these theories and explain why you believe it to be the most plausible.

KN
CO
AP
AN
SY

3. On a time line, chart the creation, rise, major achievements, decline, and destruction of the Egyptian, Maya, and Minoan civilizations. In what ways are these civilizations similar? In what ways are they different? What cultural and environmental factors might account for these differences?

AN
SY
EV

4. Some scholars have suggested that a volcanic eruption and earthquake brought an end to Minoan civilization. Earthquakes are common in that part of the world, and the Minoans had experienced them before. Archaeological evidence suggests that the Minoans had been forced to repair and rebuild damaged palaces and devastated cities many times during their tenancy on Crete. It is hard to believe that a familiar disaster ended Minoan civilization. Theorize about what factors might have made the Minoans less able or less willing to recover from this earthquake or about what other, unfamiliar or unexpected, disaster might have brought an end to their remarkable civilization. Where possible, offer evidence to support your theories.

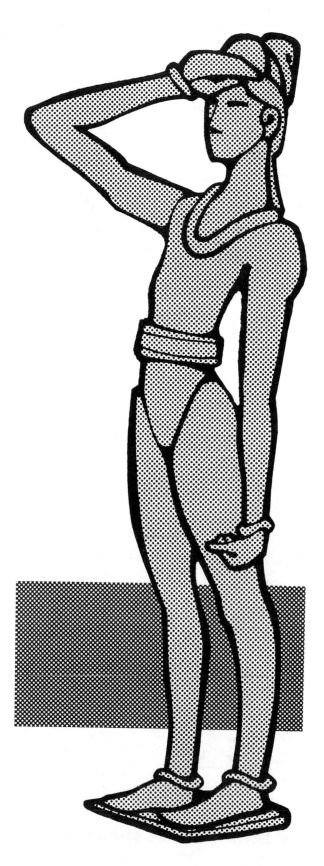

Correlated Activities

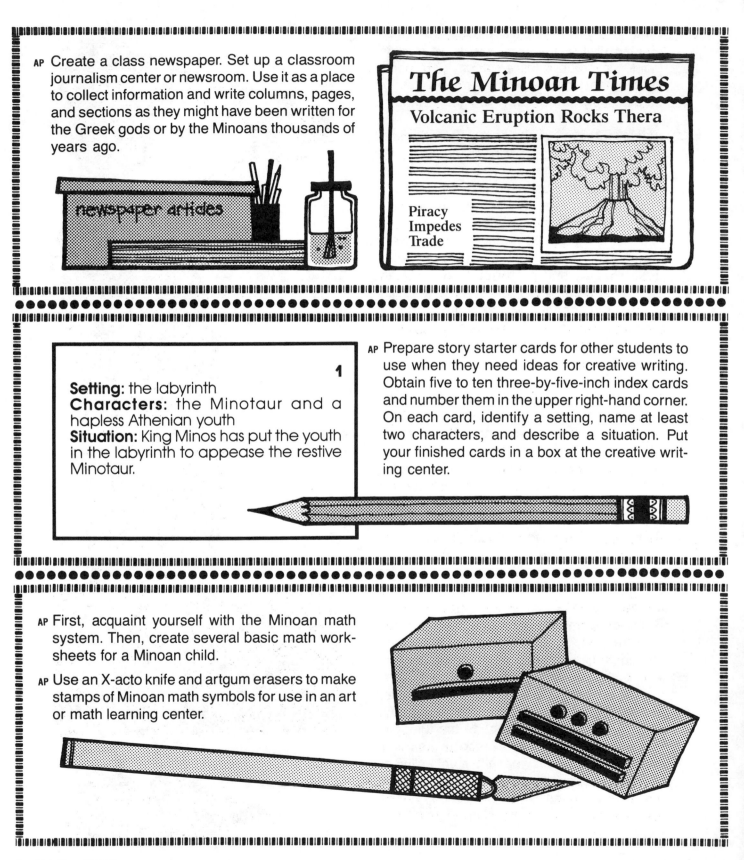

AP Create a class newspaper. Set up a classroom journalism center or newsroom. Use it as a place to collect information and write columns, pages, and sections as they might have been written for the Greek gods or by the Minoans thousands of years ago.

newspaper articles

The Minoan Times

Volcanic Eruption Rocks Thera

Piracy Impedes Trade

1

Setting: the labyrinth
Characters: the Minotaur and a hapless Athenian youth
Situation: King Minos has put the youth in the labyrinth to appease the restive Minotaur.

AP Prepare story starter cards for other students to use when they need ideas for creative writing. Obtain five to ten three-by-five-inch index cards and number them in the upper right-hand corner. On each card, identify a setting, name at least two characters, and describe a situation. Put your finished cards in a box at the creative writing center.

AP First, acquaint yourself with the Minoan math system. Then, create several basic math worksheets for a Minoan child.

AP Use an X-acto knife and artgum erasers to make stamps of Minoan math symbols for use in an art or math learning center.

Correlated Activities
(continued)

AP Cultural Exchange. Obtain fifty three-by-five-inch index cards and divide them into two equal sets. On each card in one set, write the name of an object or activity that was important to or typical of ancient Minoan culture. For example, you might include **bull-leaping, caves, double ax, leather slippers, ornate jewelry, running water (plumbing),** and **sailing vessels.** On each card in the other set, write the name of an object or activity that is important to or typical of modern culture. For example, you might include **airplanes, automobiles, fast food, football games, freeways, paper plates,** and **running water (plumbing).**

Divide the class into two teams. Give each team one set of cards. Have the teams take turns drawing cards and trying to explain the named features of their culture to members of the other team. Or have members of one team name a category (for example, **transportation** or **recreation**) for which members of the other team must supply an object or activity that is typical of their culture (for example, **sailing vessel** or **bull-leaping**). To make the game more challenging, set a limit on response time.

AP Cretan Challenge or Minoan March. Create a board game based on what you have learned about the Minoans and their life on Crete. The purpose of the game might be to escape from the heart of the labyrinth or to move from a ship in a Cretan port to the palace at Knossos without being discovered and destroyed by the robot Talos. The board might include both long pathways and shortcuts. Movement along these pathways might be controlled by the roll of dice or the spin of a spinner and complicated by **help** and **hazard** cards.

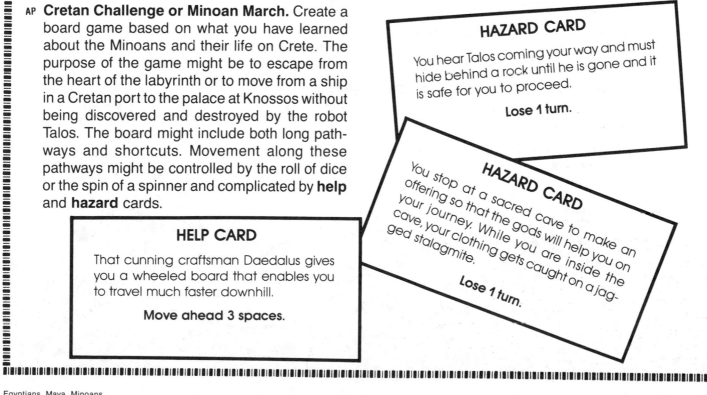

HAZARD CARD

You hear Talos coming your way and must hide behind a rock until he is gone and it is safe for you to proceed.

Lose 1 turn.

HAZARD CARD

You stop at a sacred cave to make an offering so that the gods will help you on your journey. While you are inside the cave, your clothing gets caught on a jagged stalagmite.

Lose 1 turn.

HELP CARD

That cunning craftsman Daedalus gives you a wheeled board that enables you to travel much faster downhill.

Move ahead 3 spaces.

Posttest

Circle the letter beside the best answer or the most appropriate response.

1. According to mythology, what Greek god was born in a cave on Crete?
   a. Poseidon
   b. Zeus
   c. Cronos
   d. Hades

2. According to archaeological evidence, civilization began on Crete around
   a. 6000 B.C.
   b. 3000 B.C.
   c. 1470 B.C.
   d. A.D. 1893.

3. The original settlers of Crete came from
   a. Egypt.
   b. Greece.
   c. eastern Europe.
   d. western Asia.

4. To establish safe trading routes for their surplus goods, the descendants of these settlers had to
   a. learn to sail.
   b. sign trade agreements.
   c. fight and conquer pirates.
   d. build better roads.

5. The legendary king who ruled Crete was named
   a. Daedalus.
   b. Odysseus.
   c. Minos.
   d. Thucydides.

6. This king employed a "cunning craftsman" named
   a. Daedalus.
   b. Icarus.
   c. Minotaur.
   d. Thucydides.

7. Talos was
   a. a computer.
   b. a sedimentary rock.
   c. the son of Daedalus.
   d. a robot.

8. The Minoans left offerings for their deities in
   a. temples.
   b. caves.
   c. mosques.
   d. synagogues.

9. Brave and athletic Minoan youths participated in
   a. the Olympics.
   b. pok-a-tok.
   c. bull-leaping.
   d. senet.

10. Paintings done on walls or ceilings in wet plaster are called
    a. frescoes.
    b. friezes.
    c. collages.
    d. masterpieces.

Answer Key

Pretest, Page 76

1. d	6. c
2. a	7. a
3. c	8. c
4. d	9. a
5. b	10. d

Posttest, Page 108

1. b	6. a
2. a	7. d
3. d	8. b
4. c	9. c
5. c	10. a

This is to certify that

_____

(name of student)

has satisfactorily completed a unit of study
on the

Minoans

and has been named

a

Master of the Cs—Cretan Civilization and Culture

in recognition of this accomplishment

_____

(signature of teacher)

_____

(date)

List of Related Names, Places, and Terms

Names

Aegeus
Akhenaton
Algonquians
Amemait
Amenhotep IV
Amon-Ra
Androgeos
Anubis
Ariadne
Aten
Bacabs
Brinton, D. G.
Catherwood, Frederick
Chac
Chac Mool
Champollion, Jean François
Cheops (Khufu)
Columbus, Christopher
Córdoba, Francisco
Cortés, Hernán
Cronos
Cyclopes
Daedalus
Demeter

Egyptians
Evans, Sir Arthur
Gaea
Geb
Hapi
Hatshepsut
Healy, Giles G.
Hera
Hestia
Horus
Hunab Ku
Icarus
Illiad
Imhotep
Isis
Itzamna
Khufu (Cheops)
Leonardo da Vinci
Maat
Maudslay, Alfred P.
Maya
Minoans
Minos

Minotaur
Narmer
Nepthys
Nut
Odyssey
Olmecs
Osiris
Pasiphae
Poseidon
Ra
Rhea
Ruz Lhuillier, Alberto
Sekhmet
Set
Stephens, John Lloyd
Talos
Theseus
Thoth
Thucydides
Titans
Tutankhamon
Uranus
Zeus
Zoser

Places

Aegean Sea
Ahketaten
Arkalochori Cave
Atlantis
Bonampak
Carlsbad Caverns
Central America
Copán
Crete
Egypt
Giza
Greece

Ionian Sea
Kilauea
Knossos
Krakatoa
Luray Caverns
Mammoth Cave
Mediterranean Sea
Mesoamerica
Mexico
Mount Olympus
Mount St. Helens
Mount Vesuvius

Nevado del Ruiz
Nile River
Palenque
Paricutín
Psychro Cave
Punt
Rosetta
Santoríní (Thera)
Thebes
Thera (Santoríní)
Tikal
Yucatán Peninsula

List of Related Names, Places, and Terms
(continued)

Terms

active
aesthetic
archaeologist
architecture
artifact
artisan
ash
attribute
Bronze Age
calendar
calendrics
canopic jar
cartouche
cataracts
causeway
cenote
civilization
codex, codices
commemorate
cone
corbel
courtyard
crater
cryonics
culture
deity
democracy
divert
dormant
drought
emetic
eruption
excavate
extinct
falcon
fibula
figurine
flail
fresco
glyph
halach uinic
headdress

Hellenic
hieroglyph
hieroglyphics
hypostyle
ibis
ideogram
insignia
jaguar
labyrinth
lahar
lava
light well
limestone
loincloth
Long Count
lord chamberlain
magma
maize
mar
mastaba
Middle Kingdom
monarchy
mummification
natron
New Kingdom
New World
noxious
nuptial
obelisk
Old Kingdom
Old World
oligarchy
pahoehoe
palette
pantheon
papyrus
pharoah
pok-a-tok
polychromatic
prediction
prophecy

pylon
pyramid
quetzal
reality
regurgitate
"Ring of Fire"
robot
Rosetta stone
ruins
sarcophagus
sanctuary
sandstone
scarabaeus
scribe
scriptorium
scroll
sculpture
sedimentary
senet
shaduf
sistrum
site
spelunker
sphinx
stalactites
stalagmites
stela, stelae
step pyramid
Stone Age
symbolism
talisman
temple-pyramid
thalassocracy
theocracy
titan
totem pole
tsunami
tyrannical
uraeus
vent
vessel
vizier